CARNIVAL

Alexander Orloff

CARNIVAL
Myth and Cult

Perlinger

TO SVETLANA

for her strength and for her light
that has touched
the lives of so many

The original edition was published in 1980 under the title
"Karneval – Mythos und Kult" by Perlinger Verlag

© 1981 Alexander Orloff, Perlinger Verlag Ges. m. b. H., Brixentaler Straße 61,
6300 Wörgl (Austria)
Photography, text and layout: Alexander Orloff
Reproduction: Wagner'sche Univ.-Buchdruckerei, Innsbruck
Produced by Welsermühl, Wels
Printed on Euroart and Euroffset 150 g/m² by PWA G Hallein Papier AG
No part of this publication may be reproduced in whole or in part without permission
in writing from the publisher
ISBN 3-85399-026-6
Printed in Austria

Contents

Foreword

My first impression when looking through the photographic material and reading the manuscript of this book was one of astonishment and admiration for the author whose "Quest for the Grail" has taken him through the familiar as well as the obscure world of European and American carnival. Alexander Orloff's extensive collection of photographs alone merit considerable attention. To this day few publications on the phenomenon of carnival provide such a wealth of both visual and documentary evidence, offering the reader pause for reflection. One glance through the photographs will suffice to fill the reader with amazement at the aesthetic vision and artistic originality of these images, so many of which succeed in capturing the feverish intensity of the celebration at its climax. The splendour and the play of colour in all its nuances, the beauty of line and contour will delight the aesthete. The poet or casual reader interested in popular traditions and cults will discover a measure of truth and authenticity in these images that were not created in an artificial studio environment but rather in their true setting which is so vital to tradition.

Authenticity always implies originality. It cannot be contrived, imitated or fabricated. It not only requires originality but also the integrity and consent of the whole community cultivating the popular custom. Many of today's carnivalesque festivals comprised of bits and pieces borrowed from various unrelated traditions are artificially staged by professional promoters and tourist agencies. They are often pathetically boring, lacking the integrity and the popular participation so vital to the intensity and life of genuine tradition.

The author's choice of images seems to me very judicious. He has avoided the temptation to illustrate staged spectacles in which the role of the populace is reduced to that of the passive bystander. He does, however, include some images illustrating the depressing touristic, commercial aspects of today's carnival. But these few are eclipsed by the spontaneity of the celebration.

Many of his photographs show the sensuality and licentiousness of various new world carnivals, which were introduced by the first French, Spanish and Portugese colonists. The slave culture breathed new life into ancient European carnival, creating what seems to be a new celebration whose distant European roots pale beside the frenzied dancing, music, rhythm, mentality and aesthetics of black Africa.

Yet in spite of this infectious exuberance of the African soul which seems to efface the spirit of old world carnival, the traditional European celebrations have resisted the trend toward grand spectacle, licentious abandon and violence common to many urban celebrations and so often associated too directly with the true character of carnival. In the mountains and in many remote villages, a genuine sentiment for perpetuating authentic tradition has survived.

The heart of traditional European carnival is fraught with mystery. It is difficult, if not completely impossible for the casual witness to penetrate the secret soul of the celebration. The more serious observer must complement his impressions by making direct contact with those who enact the rituals. The touchstone of judgement determining the authenticity of tradition should be the community's degree of attachment to its particular custom.

A closer look at carnival often reveals that underlying the ritual is a fervent cohesive element representing an important, if not a major part of the community. A carnival tradition presupposes a long conditioning of the spirit. This begins in the nuclear family which is truly integrated into the community, to be further complemented by the existing infrastructures: youth groups, samba schools, cliques, bands and societies. All these groupings play a central role in maintaining a living, non-artificial tradition and are analogous to those ancient groupings of initiates found in certain so-called primitive cultures. They teach and reveal the esoteric details of the customs rarely apparent either to the superficial spectator or to the non-integrated families of the community. In such groups, a leader's attitude can by its liberal laxity or enthusiastic devotion either undermine or reinforce the edifice of tradition.

This book impressively illustrates the paramount role the mask plays in carnival through its specific originality and incredible diversity. We cannot imagine the celebration without painted faces, headdresses of wood, leather, metal or vegetable matter, without a disguise or masquerade in effect transforming the individual into another being. This no doubt will give the attentive observer pause to reflect on the remarkable significance, spacial extension and continuity of the mask and masquerade throughout the course of civilization. The French philosopher and sociologist, Roger Caillois, remarked in his work, "Les Jeux et les Hommes", that mankind has always worn the mask. This enigmatic and seemingly useless accessory is more common than the lever, bow and arrow, spear or plough. He maintains that no tool, no invention, belief, custom or institution lends such a degree of unity to mankind as does the mask. Entire peoples, while ignoring the most basic and precious utensils, have known the mask. Whole civilizations have prospered without any notion of the wheel or its potential applications, yet to them the mask was familiar.

For thousands of years we discovered and rediscovered the mask painted and carved onto the walls of prehistoric caves. We have traced its course from the most obscure primitive cultures to the highest of classical civilizations. Mask and war-paint decorating body and face for the purpose of intimidation; masks of Greek and Roman theatre and Asian and Latin-American dance incarnating divinities, demons, tricksters and buffoons; masks and costumes worn during ceremonial rituals for the initiation of the young, for funerals and festivals of Africa and Oceania; as carnival disguises worn during the traditional European cycle of festivities as a means of dissimilation, metamorphosis and depersonification of the individual. The Lamas of Tibet, the Shinto priests of Japan, the Kathakali and Yashagama pantomime dancers of India, the Shamans of the Siberian steppes, the sorcerers of black Africa, the actors of the Nô-Theatre, the dancers who in Guatamala and Mexico evoke the "Conquistas" – all disguise themselves for diversion, ritual, the ceremonial and the theatrical.

Through mass media this notion of the mask's permanence across space and time has become familiar to us. We find it defying the turbulent flux of centuries in countries where the religious beliefs have historically excluded its use. The collection of the Musée International du Carnaval et du Masque in Binche proves how misleading historic generalizations can be. In the Atlas mountains of Morocco, under the sway of the Islamic ethic, the masquerade is practiced during the Aid-el-Kabir of Ourigane. The central character of these celebrations is the ram, a zoomorphic mask often found in European custom. This magico-religious nature of the mask as manifested in the Maroccan example with its profound ritual background generally holds true for the masks used in the traditional ceremonies of Oceania, Africa and Asia.

The world of European carnival presents a certain unity as well. Parallel currents traverse our countries in spite of political and ethnic diversity. Yet many customs practiced in the same manner appear North to South, from the Ural mountains to the Atlantic coast. The same characters with identical ritual implements are to be found nearly everywhere.

A brief historical survey of the mask leads to the conclusion that at the root of our European masquerades, particularly those celebrated during the winter to spring seasonal cycle (harvest, Christmas, New Year's, carnival) there exists something other than a simple need for recreation or diversion. Though it is evident that certain large urban carnivals contain both the element of recreation and diversion, distracting man and allowing him to vent the pent up pressures of modern life, this does not explain the persistent impulse to perpetuate tradition, a tradition so replete with primitive masks, ancient proverbs, beliefs and superstitions, again and again bearing witness to our deep-rooted instinct for ritual. For this reason the Catholic Church has always regarded and fought the masquerade as a vestige of paganism.

As Roger Caillois points out, man acceeds to history and civilization the moment he rejects the mask or repudiates it as a vehicle of his innermost and collective terror. Once the mask has been stripped of its central and institutional function, it ceases to frighten him. He no longer regards it with fear and veneration, but rather as a curiosity to be admired.

DR. SAMUEL GLOTZ
Musée International du Carnaval
et du Masque–Binche

Chaos, or the Origin of the World
18th century engraving

"Dionysic stirrings arise either through the influence of those narcotic potions of which all primitive races speak in their hymns, or through the powerful approach of spring, which penetrates with joy the whole frame of nature. So stirred the individual forgets himself completely ... For a brief moment we become ourselves, the primal Being, and we experience its insatiable hunger for existence. Now we see the struggle, the pain, the destruction of appearances, as necessary, because of the constant proliferation of forms pushing into life, because of the extravagant fecundity of the world will. We feel the furious prodding of this travail in the very moment in which we become one with the immense lust for life and are made aware of the eternity and indestructibility of that lust."

FRIEDRICH NIETZSCHE

Time outside of Time

THE MYTHOLOGICAL ORIGIN OF CARNIVAL

With the yearly return of the sun from its distant appointed round with the winter solstice a mystical dance of life explodes into a spectacularly sensual kaleidoscopic frenzy of light, sound, motion and colour, plunging the senses into a chaotic spiral, down to their seething primal depths.

In a maelstrom of confetti, streamers and sequins, a flood of masqueraders, eyes ecstatically brimming with joyous abandon, transformed by the alchemy of mask and fantasy, come spilling onto once peaceful streets and avenues.

Nothing can resist this tidal wave of juggernauting chaos as it turns our ordered world on its head. No barricades can protect the precious illusions called reality, morality, piety and reason from this rip-tide of anarchy and madness where scandal, erotic license, merciless satire and profane parody prevail.

This is the realm of folly where the harlequin, the fool, the village idiot, the buffoon is king and all bow to his reign of absurdity. This insanity infects us all, whirling us through the streets, pulling down the fragile facades of our carefully constructed self images, our most sacred institutions and most respected customs. Mock tribunals presided over by masked fools judge our institutions and their leaders exposing and condemning their hypocrisies, corruption and incompetence. The world order collapses, engulfed by darkness where evil phantoms lurk.

Mischief grips us, violent passions errupt, possessed, we glimpse the dark side of our souls revealing a destructiveness never imagined. Mesmerized, reeling in trance, dancing wildly to the deafening roar of drums, bells, cymbols and flutes, our spirits soar. Briefly abandoning ourselves to the irresistible call we surface spontaneously, liberated, like millions of possessed souls we burst into the blinding brilliance of ecstatic joy, floating on the intoxicating effervescence of free form madness.

For this is a magical time outside of time in which one and all are changed, everything is reversed, inverted backward, inside out, a period of paradox where opposites unite, where order is disorder, harmony dissonance, where profanity is sacred, where no laws and no taboos are valid. This is a time of excess, overflowing emotions, unrestrained folly, joy and anger, kindness and cruelty—a mad fleeting moment where life phrenetically embraces death in a sacred dance of creation.

This is carnival time whose roots lie buried in the primordial mists of our ancestral memories far beyond history, when man lived in nature, and the gods dwelled among the mortals who worshipped them. This was an idyllic age when legend and myth revealed a greater reality, the secrets of nature and the mysteries of the cosmos.

The story found in the Pyramid texts reveals that the earth god Keb seduced the sky goddess Nut, wife of Ra, the almighty sun god. When Ra discovered their intrigue, he placed a curse on his unfaithful wife, condemning her never to give birth either in any month or in any year. The wily god Thoth detected a flaw in Ra's curse and devised a clever plan to outwit the sun god. He challenged the moon goddess to a game of draughts and winning easily asked as his prize the seventieth part of every day in the year. Out of these fractions he collected five new days and added them to the old lunar calendar of 360 days. Since these new days were not part of any month or any year, the sky goddess gave birth to five children without contradicting the sun god's curse. On the first day Osiris was born, followed by Horus, Set, Isis and, on the final day, Nephthys. The Egyptians believed that these five days stood apart from the ordinary course of time and were not fit for serious business. They came between the end of the old year and the beginning of the new.

Millenia later, we mortals of the twentieth century, children of the atomic age who have long since evicted the primordial gods of our ancestors, still find ourselves irresistibly drawn by their incredible mythological legacy. These timeless myths have survived centuries upon centuries of historical interpretations, religious manipulation and distortion only to rise again from the debris of crumbled civilizations and the ashes of expired religions. They surface and resurface–as Jung put it–in our collective subconscious because they hold the secret answers to the profound mysteries of the universe. Mythology is the very soul of our civilization. The supernatural fascination it holds for us requires our uncomprehending participation in primeval rituals, the vital energy of which continues to pulsate in our subconscious psyche during magical moments between time, between dimensions, in the cosmic chaos that preceeded creation.

When we primal creatures climbed out of the trees and caves, we began to live on the land, to grow crops, to herd animals and to gather into clans and tribes. Our lives became patterned and organized, and we began to take notice of the seasonal cycles and how much our well-being depended on their regular progression. We were awed by the mysterious capriciousness of nature and discovered that the elements of nature behaved very much as we did–with passionate anger and violence, cold indifference and cruelty, with gentle warmth, nurturing abundance and generosity. The elements had personalities which we abstracted into spirit entities with specific characteristics and powers. Eventually these spirits–the moon, the sun, the stars–became gods and demigods. When the life-giving sun god disappeared in the winter skies we saw that our world halted in its course and that the forces of life appeared to die. When the sun returned in the spring, it brought our world back to life. 16

Plants revived, animals multiplied. We rejoiced, for life was secure again. At this critical moment in the seasonal cycle, life and death appeared to be locked in an elemental struggle the outcome of which was to determine our welfare. To ensure our victory, or at least to assist the gods in their work, we devised a system of magic. We believed that if we mimicked the acts of nature by dramatically representing the actions of the gods, we could manipulate the natural forces.

To perform this magic we chose the wisest among us to communicate with the gods. We gave them divine powers making them living gods. They became god-priests or god-kings, responsible for performing all the necessary ritual magic to ensure our well-being. We performed sacred dances to bring the rain, to awaken the spring, to drive out evil. To call the sun we carried golden spheres, to promote fertility we performed ritual marriages of the sky and the earth gods. To ensure the vitality of our communities, our leaders, our crops, herds and women we made sacrifices to the gods.

The divine priests and kings were the principal actors in these magic dramatizations. The cast played the roles of decaying and dying vegitation, of life's waning powers in winter, of the renewal and resurrection of these forces with the coming of spring. Masks were used to impersonate the deities and the powerful spirits of our dead ancestors who had direct contact with the gods.

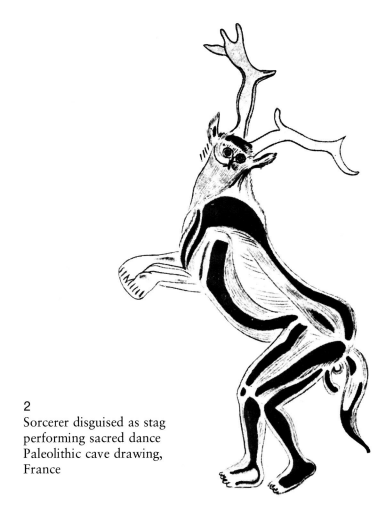

2
Sorcerer disguised as stag performing sacred dance Paleolithic cave drawing, France

The power of the mask enabled our magicians to transcend their own beings and become one with the gods. In this cosmic drama the priest-king, who represented the faltering forces of nature in winter, would perish with the coming of spring.

The advent of winter signalled that the divinity of the priest-king was faltering. This weakness was very dangerous for us, and we regarded it as the reason for our misfortunes during the previous year. We heaped all our ill luck on the priest-king and made him the scapegoat. As winter lost its battle with the newborn spring, so too our old king would lose the ritual battle with the new incarnation. He would be sacrificed as the scapegoat, thus redeeming our community and our lives. His resurrection represented the birth of the new year and the regeneration of life in the seasonal cycle.

Fertility and Ecstasy

ORIGINS OF THE CULT OF CARNIVAL

The Cult of Osiris in Egypt

Osiris, the son born to the sky goddess, was one of the great gods of antiquity who embodied the creative forces of life, fertility and vegitation. His death and resurrection were celebrated annually throughout ancient Egypt. Osiris brought cilvilization to Egypt and taught the primitive Egyptians how to cultivate cereals, corn and fruit. Having performed these miracles, Osiris entrusted his kingdom to his sister, Isis, and set out to spread his teachings throughout the world. Isis discovered wheat and barley and introduced the alphabet.

When Osiris returned to Egypt to reclaim his throne, he fell victim to a plot hatched by his evil brother Set. During the joyous homecoming celebrations, Set tricked his brother, luring Osiris into a long coffer which he then sealed and threw into the Nile. Isis, who had also become Osiris' wife, lamenting his death sailed the great river in search of the coffer. She eventually found it entwined inside a great tree. After much difficulty she recovered the body of Osiris and sailed away. On the fateful night of a full moon, she left her ship unattended and the evil Set came upon it while hunting a wild boar. Set recognized his brother's body and tore it to pieces, scattering the limbs over the land.

Upon her return, Isis discovered the horrible fate of her brother's corpse and again set sail to collect the limbs of Osiris' dismembered body. She found all but the genitals which had been eaten by the fish. Taking the remaining limbs, she fashioned waxen images of them and distributed these waxen replicas to the priests, instructing them to bury the limbs in temple graves and to worship Osiris as a god.

The lamentations of Isis and Nephthys over the torn body of their brother were heard by the sun god Ra who sent the jackel-headed god Anubis to help them piece the broken body back together. With the help of Anubis, her sister and brother Nephthys and Thoth, and her son Horus, Isis performed the sacred Egyptian rites for the dead. She fanned the corpse wrapped in linen with her great wings, and Osiris revived. From that day on Osiris became Lord of the Underworld and ruled over the dead.

The divine passion of Osiris was reenacted annually at a great spring festival around the time of the winter solstice during the five special days outside of time. The historian Herodotus recounts the events of these celebrations in which the people mourned Osiris by beating their breasts and showing deep sorrow for their dead god. A great wooden bull with a huge golden sun held in its horns was pulled on a barge which rolled on wheels. This was the bull Apis who had helped Osiris discover agriculture, and the barge on wheels was a replica of the ship on which Isis had sailed in search of her brother's body. A ritual marriage of Isis and Osiris was performed after which a virgin, beautifully dressed as the bride, was thrown into the Nile to consecrate the union of the fertile waters of the river with the land.

At night a torch-lit procession was held accompanied by masked priests representing the other divinities, Horus, Thoth, Anubis and the spirits of the dead ancestors over whom Osiris ruled. The streets of the town were lit by torches so that the spirits who rose with Osiris could easily find their way to the offerings of food laid out for them outside their old homes. The Egyptians believed their ancestral spirits to have great power over the earth as they dwelled in its depths. These souls were capable of affecting the fertility of the soil, therefore enlisting their good will was extremely important. In some villages the processions included a golden casket carried by priests proclaiming that Osiris had been found. Images of the dead god were modelled out of earth and corn and then buried to be dug up sprouting corn shoots the following agricultural festival.

Since Osiris represented the creative energies, his processions included images of genitals carried by women who sang obscene songs to promote fertility. In some places Osiris was played by a red-haired priest or actor, the colour of the hair symbolizing the colour of corn. At the end of the festival, the

Isis and her sacred barge
The base epoch, Egypt

3

red-haired incarnation of the corn spirit was ritually sacrificed, dismembered or burned. His limbs or ashes were then scattered over the fields in sacred ploughing and sowing ceremonies.

The ritual theatrical presentations of seasonal cycles, the decay and growth of vegetation, the life and death struggle of nature's elemental forces and the reinvigoration of the god-king were all integral parts of community life. Cult rituals were performed not only to ensure the fertility of women, cattle and crops, but also to revitalize community spirit and reinvest its members and leaders with the vitality of the new year. The dramatic death and resurrection of the benevolent god who sacrificed his life for the welfare of his people was the magic re-enactment of nature's eternal cycle of renewal.

Apis, the sacred bull, carrier of the sun
The base Epoch, Egypt

4

Cult rituals celebrating the resurrection of life can be found across the face of the earth, from the great Mayan and Aztec civilizations of South and Central America to the ancient Hindu and Chinese cultures of the East, among the African tribes and in the northern latitudes of pagan Europe. These apparently unrelated cultures developed remarkably parallel mythologies from what appears to be a nearly universal philosophical interpretation of nature's cosmic mysteries. God-kings who descend from the heavens to live among man and to reveal nature's secret wonders appear again and again in sacred texts, hieroglyphic writings and mondithic sculptures as the giant architects of our ancient civilizations.

The Celebrations of the Near East

In Mesopotamia, the cradle of our civilization, the Eastern Mediterranean region, the Aegean and throughout western Asia similarities in mythology and cult rituals were more pronounced. The cultures of these areas overlapped and borrowed freely from each other.

One of the legends of southern Babylonia tells of the young Sumerian god Tammuz, the lover of the mother goddess Ishtar. According to the legend, Tammuz died and descended to the world of the dead. Ishtar followed her lover to the nether world. In her absence love's passion died, life stopped and mankind was menaced by extinction. Ishtar was allowed to sprinkle the water of life on her dead lover. Tammuz revived, and upon their return to the upper world nature came back to life. A wild new year's festival called the *Zakmuk* celebrated the revival of Tammuz. During the *Zakmuk* the king was required to humiliate himself and appear in front of the god Marduk in order to reinvigorate his powers and renew his claim to the throne.

The ancient Persians celebrated a five day new year's festival called the *Sacaea* or *The ride of the one-eyed beardless buffoon*. A deformed man, usually a condemned criminal, was chosen as a mock king to represent the faltering old year. He was a substitute for

20

the real king who abdicated for the five days. In antiquity, the king himself had to play this role.

The mock king, or "Zoganes", rode through the streets of the city stripped naked on a mule. In one hand he held a fan and complained of the unbearable heat, while jeering crowds drenched him with cold water and pelted him with ice and snow. *The ride of the one-eyed beardless buffoon* was supposed to drive out the winter.

After his ride he was dressed in the king's regal robes and crowned. The "Zoganes" reigned supreme and all the privileges of the king were granted him, including use of the royal harem. During the festivities slaves were freed and their masters were obliged to serve them. The deformed king was also attended by the real king in a procession through the streets of the city during which the substitute king issued ridiculous orders. He had the right to demand gifts from the rich and to confiscate goods from the merchants. Those who refused would be sprayed with foul liquid or pelted with mud. The day before the end of his reign he was ritually married to the goddess Ishtar, played by a priestess of the cult. On the final day of the *Sacaea* the "Zoganes" was stripped of the king's robes, beaten and put to death.

During this year-end revelry, a more solemn ten day celebration was also held. The *Hamaspathaidaya* commemorated the spirits of the dead ancestors who rose from the nether world to avenge injustices committed during the year. Large banquets were held, special offerings of food were placed on their graves. Offerings of drinks were placed on the roofs of houses as it was believed that the spirits avenging injustices could raise the roof and create havoc if they were not properly appeased.

The Jews celebrated a similar year-end festival called the *Purim,* adopted from the Babylonian tradition.

The book of Esther refers to it, dating the celebration around the 3rd or 4th century B. C. The *Purim* was described as a drunken rout which defied all the laws of Moses. Grotesque masks were worn, rabbis were ridiculed and mocked. All taboos were lifted and men and women exchanged dress. A contest between two rivals for the title of king was held in which the loser, called the "Haman", was crucified. In later accounts of this custom effigies were burned as a substitute for the human sacrifice.

In Syria and on Cyprus the death and resurrection theme again appears dating back to the 7th century, B. C. Here the central characters are Adonis and Aphrodite as well as Attis and Cybele. Attis too was associated with reviving vegitation. He was the beloved of Cybele, the goddess of fertility. Their worship was particularly wild with blood sacrifices, frenzied dancing to the music of clashing cymbals, drums and flutes. At the height of the ecstatic rites, the priests of Attis would slash each other with knives, spraying the blood over the altar of the temple. The ritual climaxed with the castration of one of the priests, after which masquerading people danced and rejoiced in an uncontrolled orgiastic celebration.

The Cult of Dionysus

The Homeric hymn to Demeter reveals the Eleusian mysteries of the Greek myths from the 7th century B. C. In the legend of Demeter, the grieving mother and her lost daughter constitute the core of the myth.

While gathering flowers, the young Persephone was kidnapped by Pluto, the Lord of the Underworld. Demeter desperately searched for her missing daughter. When she learned from the sun that Pluto had taken Persephone to Hades, Demeter, the corn goddess, cursed the seeds and vowed never to let the corn sprout until her daughter was released. Seeing that the land was barren, Zeus learned of Demeter's curse and intervened, commanding the release of Persephone on the condition that she remain in the underworld as Pluto's bride for one third of the year. When Persephone returned from Hades, the corn sprouted, flowers bloomed and mankind rejoiced.

The festivals honouring Demeter began with fasting and long vigils, torch-light processions dramatizing the disappearance, lamentation and the search for the missing Persephone. Pigs, associated with Demeter because of their apparent fertility, were sacrificed to the goddess. Great rejoicing, dancing, drinking, ribald joking and lewd games climaxed the celebration. On some islands the festival ended with a ritual re-enactment of Persephone's disappearance into the underworld. Pigs, pine branches and cakes of dough were thrown into deep chasms and later collected and planted with the corn.

Of all the gods of the Greek pantheon, Dionysus, or Bacchus, epitomized the ancient mystic legacy of orgiastic fertility rites. Today the word *Bacchanalia* still describes the wild cult of this god of life, of joyous sensual liberation, the god of wine, music, art, theatre and dance, the god of creative madness. His myth is told by the great epic poets, philosophers and historians–Plato, Herodotus, Plutarch, Homer.

Dionysus was the god of the vine, of fruit trees and he was believed to have first yoked oxen to the plough. His legend tells that he was born twice. Zeus mated with Persephone and she bore him a horned child, Zagreus, or Dionysus. The infant was quick and clever. One day he climbed his father's great throne and seized the lightning of Zeus. While on the throne the infant god was attacked by the Titans who had distracted him with a mirror and a rattle. But Dionysus was a trickster, he had the power to change form at will. First he assumed the shape of Zeus, then changed himself into a young man, a lion, a serpent, a horse and a bull. It was in the form of a bull that the Titans caught him and hacked him to pieces.

There are various versions of this myth. One tells that Zeus raised his young son, ate his heart and conceived Dionysus again by Semele, a mortal. During her pregnancy Semele was seized by an irresistible urge to dance whenever she heard the music of the flute, and the unborn Dionysus danced with her. After the birth Semele perished in the fire from the lightning cast by Zeus and descended to Hades. Dionysus also descended to Hades in search of his mother and thus became known as a god of the underworld. On his return, he emerged from beneath the sea bringing the spring with him.

Legend tells that Dionysus was born by Semele purely as a source of joy to mankind. The coming of his black ship accross the sea was an ecstatic event in Thrace on the Greek mainland, where the origin of the myth dates back to the 8th century B. C. Here the cult of Dionysus became most popular among the oppressed social elements, the women and the slaves, particularly after the Thracians were absorbed in the dominant Helenistic culture.

In his *Bacchae,* Euripides tells how the arrival of Dionysus was heralded by miracles.

5
The voyage of Dionysus
Painting on the inside of an Exekias bowl, 6th century BC.

The earth flowed with milk, wine and honey. Grapes ripened on the vine in a single day.

Orgiastic cult festivals were celebrated between the winter solstice and the vernal equinox. A replica of Dionysus' ship on wheels was pulled through the streets followed by a wild procession. Musicians played flutes, cymbols, drums and rattles. Their phrenetic music, both harmonic and dissonant, drove the people to ecstatic heights of joy. On his ship, Dionysus, played by a priest of the cult, was represented by a bearded two-faced mask crowned with grape clusters and holding a scepter or "Thyrsus", tipped with the sacred pine cone. The ship carried the sacred wine which liberated the senses.

In Homer's *Iliad,* Dionysus was said to have risen from the fabled underwater grotto of the sea nymph Thetis who fed him the food of the gods and made him immortal. His sea

23

The Procession of Bacchus
17th century engraving

6

cart was accompanied by an entourage of nymphs, satyres, nude dancers singing lusty songs and a host of masquerading incarnations of the god—bulls, calves, pigs, asses and a chorus of goats. Dionysus was attended by his consorts, the Menaides, who paraded with huge phalluses. In the ecstatic frenzy that surrounded the ship, women would approach to be flogged, an ancient ritual believed to promote fertility and also symbolizing communion with the spirits of the dead. At night the Menaides, re-enacting Dionysus' flight from the Titans, would go off into the mountains, capture a live bull, tear it apart and eat the raw flesh. In antiquity, they also cast lots to chose whose first-born would be sacrificed as the infant Dionysus. In Thrace, even grown men were torn to pieces by the frenzied Menaides. Legend tells that the Thracian king Lykourgos opposed Dionysus and prevented the vegitation from sprouting. The god struck the king with madness and the Menaides tore him to pieces. The sacrifice of the animals which were believed to be incarnations of the horned god, and the eating of the raw flesh was a solemn sacrament as was the drinking of the sacred wine.

During the festival of *Anthesteria,* held in February, pine trees, sacred to Dionysus, were burned. The arrival of the rolling ship from which volleys of figs, nuts and small pastries were thrown to the crowds, heralded the beginning of the sacred wine-mixing ceremony. Casks of the new sacramental wine were opened, drinking contests were held in which the remainder of each pitcher consumed had to be poured out on the ground as an offering to Dionysus.

The marriage of Dionysus and Ariadne was celebrated with wild feasting. This ritual marriage was believed to promote the fertility of plant and animal life. The orgiastic festivities closed with a *Feast of Pots,* dedicated to the dead souls who rose from the underworld during these days of celebration to right the injustices committed in the community during the year. Pots of cooked vegetables and grains were set out as offering and appeasements to these "Keres", some of which had malevolent natures. Masked representatives of these spirits had the right to demand gifts from members of the commun-

24

ity. Those who refused risked chastisement by the masked spirits, including unhooking doors, putting out the hearth, fouling the well or raising the roof. At the end of the festival the people chased the spirits away from their homes with branches of hawthorn, yelling, "Begone ye Keres, Anthesteria is over."

The Kalends of Ancient Rome

In ancient Italy this joyous year-end cycle of festivals was also celebrated from the winter solstice to the vernal equinox. Like the Greek, Near Eastern and Egyptian rites, these too were linked to the ritual agricultural preparations for the spring sowing and planting. These festivals were dedicated to the gods associated with the regeneration of nature's forces in the new year. The 1st of January marked the *Kalends* venerating Janus, the two-faced god and his entourage of lesser woodland spirits. Masquerading satyres, pans and wood nymphs danced in an atmosphere of drunken abandon. People disguised themselves in the skins of various wild animals—stags, goats, pigs and wolves. Men and women exchanged dress. Erotic songs were sung, bawdy games were played and gifts were exchanged. The *Kalends* continued to be celebrated throughout the Roman Empire well into the Christian era. The festive season culminated in the month of February, which derives its name from the latin word Februum, literally, instrument of purification. February was the last month of the Roman year during which the injustices and ill fortunes of the old year were purged. In February, the pastoral *Lupercalia,* or wolf festival, was celebrated. Plutarch tells that during this celebration two youths engaged in a ritual competition. Cakes made of flour from the previous harvest were offered. Several goats and a dog were sacrificed. The youths smeared the blood from the knife used in the sacrifice on each other's foreheads. The blood was then wiped off with a piece of wool dipped in milk. Ovid theorized that the dramatization represented death and originally included human sacrifice. The wiping off of the blood with milk-soaked wool symbolized the renewal of life. The youths, naked except for the wreaths on their heads, then wrapped themselves in the skins of the sacrificed animals and let out a laugh as a sign of revival.

A great banquet was held after which the competition began. Two groups led by each of the youths engaged in a footrace. During this race, young women crowded near the runners to recieve lashes from the "Februa", long strips of hide cut from the skins of the sacrificed animals. The lashings, an act of ritual fertilization similar to the Greek custom, was supposed to help the women conceive and safely deliver their children.

The masked "Lupercali" became possessed by the divinity Fauna, the mischievous spirit

of the woods conceived in goat-form, who had the power to ward off wolves and to cause herds and crops to flourish. The ritual was one of purification and protection believed to promote the fecundity of the herd. The foot-race was a symbolic race to catch the spring. The *Lupercalia* continued to be celebrated in Rome to the very end of the 5th century A. D.

The *Parentalia*, like the Greek *Anthisteria*, honoured the dead ancestors. Masked processions representing the dead souls made their way through the city streets collecting special offerings which were given to atone for any injustices inflicted during the year. The *Parentalia* also survived well into the Christian era. In the 5th century Pope Gelasius I replaced the ancient pagan celebration with a Christian version, *the Purification of the Virgin Mary*.

The most widely celebrated festival of the Roman calendar was the *Saturnalia*. There is some controversy surrounding the dates on which the original *Saturnalia* was celebrated in antiquity. The noted ethnologist, Sir James Frazer, whose remarkable work,

26

"The Golden Bough" is the source for much of the mythological heritage of ancient carnivals described here, theorized that the *Saturnalia* may have been celebrated in February culminating the old year of the ancient Roman calendar. In Roman antiquity, the old calendar underwent numerous adjustments, accommodating lunar and solar cycles. Eventually the *Saturnalia,* at least in Rome, became fixed to the winter solstice in mid December.

The great poet Virgil glorified Saturn or Saturnus the beneficent king of Latium as a civilizer of man, a law giver who gathered the mountain people of Italy and taught them to work the land, to plant and to sow. Temples to Saturn date to the 5th century B. C. Seneca described the *Saturnalia* as a mad pursuit of pleasure. Slaves were set free for the seven days of the festival. They exchanged roles and clothes with their masters and were given the right to criticize and to ridicule them. The inversion of rank included the highest officials who relinquished their state duties to slaves wearing togas. A mock king was elected by lots and temporarily ruled the insane, upside down world which symbolized the idyllic Golden Age of Saturn when men were equal and nature so bountiful that no one had to work.

During the *Saturnalia,* gifts were exchanged. The people drank excessively, danced wildly, masqueraded and blackened their faces, played pranks and bawdy games. Small figurines made of clay in the image of the god were thrown around. A burlesque king, dressed in the red robes symbolic of Saturn, gave inane orders to his court of noblemen. At the end of his reign, the substitute king was put to death. When the Roman Republic was established, the execution of the Saturnalian king was abolished, at least in the city of Rome itself, and effigies were used for the ritual sacrifice. Accounts of Christian monks show that the custom continued to exist in the remote regions of the Roman Empire as late as the 4th century A. D.

Christ's own passion may have figured in the *Saturnalia* celebrated by the Roman legions stationed in Jerusalem. In remote outposts of the Empire, far from the civilizing influence of Rome, traditional festivals were often celebrated according to old customs and ancient calendars. The Roman legions may have held their *Saturnalia,* or a version of it that also corresponded to the Jewish *Purim* in the spring. Christ's procession in the red robe and crown of thorns through the jeering crowds of Jerusalem bears the characteristics of both the Roman and the Jewish celebration. His crucifiction as King of the Jews bears resemblance to the sacrifice of the "Haman" in Jewish tradition as well as to the execution of the burlesque king of the Roman *Saturnalia.*

As P. Wendland points out in his essay, "Jesus als Saturnalienkönig", a theme adopted by Frazer, Pontius Pilot, when choosing the mock king from among condemned criminals, may have been compelled to choose the rebel Christ to play the tragic king of this ancient carnival. Christ's dramatic death and resurrection as son and saviour is clearly a Christian adaptation of the passion plays in classical Greek, Roman, Babylonian and Egyptian mythology.

The New Year Celebrations of Pagan Europe

The expansion of the Roman Empire brought the pantheon of Roman gods into contact with the deities worshipped by other cultures. In the 3rd century B.C., the classical Roman way of life was already being diluted by these outside influences. It was in this century that the wild cult of Attis and Cybele was introduced to Rome. In the 2nd century B.C., Dionysus and his ecstatic *Bacchanals* invaded Rome. The weary Roman gods could not resist the vitality of these new cults. The rapid rise of Christianity was further proof that the process of decay had begun. Myth and cult were gradually degenerating into structured religion and politics–a development which had already been the undoing of many other civilisations.

Julius Caesar returned from his triumphs in Western Europe with more tales of strange cult rites for the gods worshipped by the Celts of Gaul. Both Caesar, in his "Gallic Wars", and later the great historian Pliny described the heathen races of the British Isles and mainland Gaul whose gods were similar to the deities of the Mediterranean region, especially the Roman pantheon.

The Celtic peoples worshipped a mother goddess who had two mates, Taranis, a sky god, and Cernunnos-Esus, a two-faced seasonal spirit, represented as half man, half stag. During the winter solstice the mother goddess would descend to the nether world to be with her second husband Cernunnos-Esus. Her first husband, Taranis, would become outraged and appeal to Smertullus the almighty, who appeared in the form of a wolf, to change Cernunnos back to Esus so that he may return to earth and bring the mother goddess with him. The corresponding cult rites included a sacred hunt for the stag who was brought back to camp and burned. The people masqueraded in deer skins and then held a week-long orgy.

The divine truth was the special province of the all-powerful Druid priests, and to record it in any way would dissipate the vitality of their religious order. Accounts of their cult rituals come from observations made by Caesar, Pliny and Posidonius, a Greek explorer who travelled in Gaul about fifty years before Caesar.

The Celts were primarily a pastoral people, and their annual cycle began in November when the herds returned from pasture. On the 1st of November, the Druid priests held

8
Ritual hunt of sorcerer and deer. The animals are both quarrey and symbols of fertility. Paleolithic cave drawing, France

a great new year's festival for Samhain, the Lord of the Dead, who represented the dark forces of the underworld which prevailed during the winter months. On *the Eve of Samhain,* the souls of all those who had died the previous year surfaced. On this night they were released from the bodies of the animals where they had been confined, to circulate briefly among the living. Processions of grotesque masked spirits led by a horse-headed sun god in white robes went from house to house. Long verses were read in praise of the sun, and offerings were collected to appease the freed souls and the ghosts, gobblins and fairies who rose with them. The fairies were believed to be the spiritis of ancient kings who surfaced at the end of the year to ensure that their old realm was in order and that injustices and disruptions which had occured during the old year were properly atoned for. To appease the masked spirits, a treat was offered. Those who failed or refused to make the necessary offering risked their vengeance.

At night, great purifying fires were burned to bless the new year and to drive out evil forces. Huge wicker cages, built in the shape of giant beings, were filled with various animals, condemned criminals and suspect-

ed witches. The Druid priests piled wood around these giant cages and set fire to them as an offering for a bountiful new year.

In 61 A.D., the Romans banned these bizarre ritual sacrifices, but the pagan rites persisted well into the Christian era. In spite of the Roman Church's condemnations, horses and oxen continued to be sacrificed in converted pagan temples, taken over by the Christians. In the 6th century A.D., Pope Gregory the Great relented, allowing animal sacrifices to continue but only under the condition that they honoured Christian saints and not pagan idols. Two centuries later, Pope Gregory IV incorporated *the Eve of Samhain* into the Church's holy calendar as *Halloween* or *All Saints Day.* In remote rural areas throughout Celtic Europe, however, many of the traditional Druid rites continued unchanged for centuries.

Further to the north, in Germanic Europe, the Romans encountered the Teutonic races and with them yet another parallel mythological heritage. Tacitus and Snorri, a Scandinavian poet historian, described myths very similar to those of the Eastern Mediterranean. The legend of Baldar the Beautiful, son of the great Odin whose death and dismemberment compared to that of

Osiris and Dionysus, is one of these. Balder fell victim to the evil Loki, a counterpart to the Egyptian Set, who plotted the death of his brother Osiris. Balder descended to the subterranean world ruled by Hela, the Germanic Persephone, goddess of the dead. Nature and the world of the living mourned Balder's passing. The divinities Nerthus, the goddess of fertility, and her daughter Freya, the protective mother goddess, are Teutonic counterparts to the Greek Demeter. Freya and her brother Frey, both creative spirits, ruled in fabled Alfhein, land of Alfar or elves who left patches of greener grass wherever they had frolicked.

The *Yule, Jul* or *Noel* festival celebrated the Teutonic new year. A Yule log was burned to commemorate the birth of the sun. Goats, cocks, pigs, horses and boars were sacrificed to the god Frey. Great banquets were prepared. Cakes baked in the shape of a boar, sacred to Frey, were served. A joyous procession pulled a ship on wheels with an image of Frey through the crowds of masqueraders disguised as bears, deer, stags and boars. Men and women inverted sex roles, sang lusty songs, made effeminate and lewd gestures, danced and drank in orgiastic revelry. Frey was ritually married to one of the priestesses attending his ship on wheels. Freya, his sister, was also drawn around on a sea wagon which was used to bless the fields before spring sowing.

The seasonal cycle in the northern latitudes was particularly dramatic since the sun truly disappeared in the winter darkness. There were only two seasons in the calendar—summer and winter. The most striking feature of the clear winter sky was the Milky Way, regarded by the northern pagans as the road of the stars which linked heaven to this world. Symbolized by the ritual marriage, the Milky Way represented the sperm of the sky god consecrating his sacred union with the earth mother.

At the time of the winter solstice, the souls of the dead circulated among the living before ascending the stellar road to heaven. As in the Celtic myth, these souls had been confined in the stomach of the hibernating bear throughout the previous year. The emergence of the bear farting after his winter hibernation signaled both the end of winter and the liberation of the souls. The world of the dead joined the world of the living during this period of feasting and celebrating.

The *Yule Fest* celebrated that decisive cosmic moment when the dead and the living joined in exalting the birth of the new year and the prosperity, fertility and regenerative power it promised. The ritual orgies of excessive drinking, eating, sexuality and masquerading stimulated the cosmic forces, woke up the spring, purified the community preparing it for the passage into the new year. Some aspects of the *Yule Fest* eventually were absorbed into the Christian Christmas tradition and survive to this day.

The Battle of the Gods

CARNIVAL AND THE CHURCH IN THE MIDDLE AGES

The beginning of the Christian era turned Europe into a whirlpool of converging myths, legends, cults and religions which streamed over the continent with the conquering Roman legions. Osiris and Isis, Dionysus, Saturnus, Attis and Cybele, Demeter, Lupus and the Faunus—all of these blended with the cult traditions of the Celts, Saxons, the Teutonic, Germanic and Scandinavian peoples. The great similarities of all their mythic cosmologies made them naturally compatible, and the various local and imported cults flourished.

The Roman Empire eventually began to export the great common denominator—Christianity. The Holy Roman Church spread its rather transparent liturgical veneer over the ancient pagan traditions, and this liturgy that had already borrowed extensively from the mythological heritage of the Mediterranean races began to assimilate European paganism. Ancient spirits, gods, cults, sacred groves and temples were rediscovered and reintegrated bearing new names and new Christian values.

The transition was not always smooth, for not all the ancient pagan traditions surrendered easily to the new religion. The Church encountered persistent resistance to its moralistic doctrines and zealous attempts to give new moral and spiritual significance to the baser aspects of the old popular myths. The ancient heritage of gross orgiastic fertility rites, cruel sacrifices, masquerading and idolatry, legends of immoral revelry, the disgraceful incestuous and impious adventures of the gods were not at all compatible with the guilt-suffering and penitent trials of the soul, required by the new god.

The history of the Middle Ages, or more accurately, the Dark Ages, with its punitive Crusades, the horrors of the Inquisition, witch hunts, exorcisms and trials by ordeal, is the sad testament of the rise of Christianity. For a thousand years and more, intolerance prevailed over enilghtenment as the new religion won over our heathen souls. The unseemlier side of the freer, nature-bound cult traditions, still practiced by the peoples under the sword of the Holy Roman Empire, became the object of violent persecution as the Holy Church attempted to substitute the moral cross for the pagan symbols and customs. Calendars were adjusted, ancient rites were banned or replaced by new festivals with different names and new trappings under the guise of Church tradition. Saints' days, complete with corresponding folklore to legitimize their presence, were superimposed on celebrations honouring ancient deities. But to no avail—the vital traditions of antiquity were too deeply entrenched in the pagan soul, they refused to die. The *Saturnalia, Bacchanalia, Lupercalia, Parentalia,* the cults of Osiris, Cybele and Attis, the *Samhain* and *Yule fests* continued to celebrate the wild year-end cycle with traditional joyous abandon and mocking irreverence. The gods were too powerful for even the great crusading armies of the new religion. The Christians were forced to withdraw from the holy war against the ancient carnivals. The Popes relented, though grudgingly, and continued their campaign of subverting the persistent paganism even as the ancient gods began to invade the Church itself.

The Feast of Fools

Ironically in the Middle Ages, while the popes waged their holy war on paganism, the spirit of carnival disguised as the fool infiltrated the Church itself. True to its ancient heritage, *the Feast of Fools* made a mockery of the solemn Christian liturgy, unmasking the hypocrisy of the pious papal campaign against the old rites.

This bizarre ecclesiastical celebration lasted the twelve days from Christmas to Epiphany. On the 26th of December, the lower clergy, subdeacons and monks, gathered in special council to elect their pope. The mock "Fool's Pope" or "Abbot of Unreason" was dressed in pontifical robes and like the Saturnalian king reigned over the inverted heirarchical order.

On the 1st of January, dedicated to the ancient god Janus, or, according to the Christians, *the Feast of the Circumcision,* this bishop of folly made his triumphant entrance into the church, heralding a period of orgiastic clerical revelry. He was joyously received by grotesquely masked members of the clergy, disguised as women and animals. Laymen impersonating nuns and monks joined in the dancing and singing of indecent songs. In the midst of all this uproarious rejoicing, the "Fool's Pope" gave inane blessings and maledictions. The altar was transformed into a banquet table around which the lower clergy sat drinking, eating greasy foods, gambling and playing dice games. Clouds of stinking incense from smouldering shoe leather filled the church.

The debauchery reached its climax on January 6th, the *Epiphany* or *Festival of the Ass.* A donkey covered with a golden canopy was led to the altar. A liturgy was sung to the glory of the animal while the choir brayed the usual chorus of halleluhias and amens. The ass was to Jesus what the boar and the bull were to Osiris and Dionysus—a symbolic representation of the god. In ancient times, the ass was considered an incarnation of the god of the jews, and the association was adapted to Christ.

A young girl carrying a child rode the animal, thus re-enacting Mary's flight into Egypt. A long parody of the holy mass was then read. The service ended with the congregation dancing around and braying like donkeys. After this sacrilegious mass, the clergy, carrying lanterns and exchanging smutty jokes and insults with the people,

Festival of Fools
France 1743

9

sailed through the crowded streets on a rolling ship of fools. The procession stopped at the houses of the rich and demanded money. This carnival parade eventually returned to the church, in front of which a makeshift stage had been constructed on which obscene farces were then presented.

Victor Hugo's novel, "The Hunchback of Notre Dame", opens with this carnival scene in which Quasimodo is being crowned king of the fools amid a festive atmosphere of laughing and jeering, onlookers watching bawdy theatrical presentations staged in front of the great cathedral. At the end of the 12th century, Pope Innocent III condemned this blasphemous celebration and described the *Feast of the Circumcision* held in Notre Dame as an abomination of shameful deeds which desecrated the holy place with obscenities and even the shedding of blood, making a shameful mockery of the clergy. Three hundred years later, the Theological Faculty of Paris was still condemning the *Festival of Fools*.

The Church was determined to expel these mischievous pagan gods who kept surfacing in the imagination of the people around the time of the winter solstice. Their appearance in the popular celebrations was lamentable enough, but their wicked presence in the hearts and minds of the clergy outraged the Church fathers.

It did not suffice that the omnipotent infallible Christian God was supreme to all other divinities, the Church still feared the old beliefs. The ancient gods were downgraded, reduced to the rank of evil spirits and demons. God, of course, was capable of saving man from these malevolent demons, but to impersonate and mimic them with animal masks and skins was dangerously close to courting the devil himself. What the Church feared most was the powerful magic of the animal mask. In the 2nd century, it began its campaign against the ancient new year festivals, deploring the *Kalends* of January as particularly scandalous.

The Roman carnivals were the most orgiastic and excessively violent. Executions of criminals were held in public as part of the festive entertainment. The cadavers of the executed would be included in macabre street processions. All social and legal restraints evaporated. Fighting, crimes of vengeance, even murder and rape were common. Vendettas against political figures were settled by assassination. The riotous street celebrations often deteriorated into brawls and pitched battles between rival groups who would throw dangerous missiles instead of the sweets, clay pellets, kernels of corn and egg shells that were eventually to become confetti. Containers of water and sewage were dumped on the heads of masquerading crowds from windows and balconies. Behind these windows, the wealthy Romans and aristocratic patricians held drunken orgies of gluttony and fornication. Some early Church fathers tragically achieved martyrdom and even sainthood in their attempt to save the immoral souls of the Romans. By the 16th century, the Church, with the help of the civil goverers, had managed to reduce the violent excess of Rome's year end celebrations.

Old Festivals – New Names

Up into the 14th century, repetitious warnings, condemnations, threats and orders poured into Church archives. Thanks to these routine diatribes, the Church fathers unwittingly preserved a historical image of Medieval European carnivals. At the end of the 7th century, a letter addressed to the Pope from St. Boniface revealed that *the Kalends* were being celebrated in the very shadow of St. Peter's in Rome. Records show that the cults of Isis and Nerthus were still being celebrated in the sacred groves of Germanic Europe until the 12th century. At the beginning of the 16th century, the Council of Ulm prohibited the use of a ship on wheels during the local carnival or Fasnacht. The Church continued to condemn the worship of the god Janus, and dioceses throughout Europe exhorted their congregations not to participate in these pagan cult rites. Inspired sermons were held on the subject of how men could pervert themselves and their masculine virility to such a degree as to dress and act like women. "How could they", asked St. Maxim in an impassioned sermon, "who were created by God in his own image, degrade themselves by mimicking wild beasts and monsters? Did they not understand that by dancing around in these sinful disguises, man was transformed and entered the blasphemous world of the demons?" St. Augustine advised that anyone caught guilty of practicing these disgusting customs should be severely chastized until he had regretted committing the sacrilege.

Subsequent Church councils ruled against decorating homes with greenery, against drinking, preparing special foods or making offerings to the dead. Dancing, singing, making sacrifices to the false pagan gods, wearing any kind of mask—whether comic, tragic or satirical, playing the old woman or invoking the cursed name of Bacchus was sinful and hostile to the christian way. Anyone who dared to commit these evil acts had abandoned God the Creator and deserved the eternal fires of hell. To atone for these transgressions, years of penance were required.

The same St. Boniface, Bishop of Mainz, who reported to the Pope on the disgraceful January celebrations in the vicinity of St. Peter's, headed a reforming synod that prohibited the custom of driving out winter, popular in so many regions of Europe. The synod instructed the brethren of the Church not to observe the pagan rites and under no circumstances to even dare look at any animal disguises, particularly the bear, a vegitation demon. None of the special foods were to be eaten, fasting and penitence was encouraged during the days of sin.

While the bishops were zealously issuing canonical condemnations, more enlightened supporters within the Church were arguing that these festivals were healthy and that the

Carnival at a court of the Middle Ages 10
Illustration from a 14th century novel, France

ancients celebrated them to vent the foolishness that was pent up in man. The Church fathers were slow to accept the wisdom of this, and for centuries after they were preoccupied with creating Christian equivalents of the pagan rites to complete the liturgical calendar. If the excesses of paganism could not be completely eradicated, they at least could be made to appear Christian. The transitional winter to spring cycle of festivities had to be anchored to the Christian version of the death and resurrection myth. This cycle began with the Celtic New Year or *Eve of Samhain* which the Church converted into *Halloween* or *All Saints Day*. The Celts and many other ancient peoples divided their year into forty-day units, based on the lunar method of reckoning time. Forty days after *the Eve of Samhain*, the

35

winter solstice took place. In the middle of the 4th century, Pope Julius I shifted the birth of Christ from January 6th to December 25th and fixed *Easter* at the vernal equinox. The *Nativity* corresponded to the birth of the young sun and replaced the *Saturnalia,* the Teutonic *Yule Fest* and the Celtic rites to the stag deity, Cernunnos.

On the 2nd of February, forty days after the winter solstice, the bear emerged from winter hibernation and released the souls of the dead. According to popular folklore, if the weather was clear when the bear appeared, he would return to his lair for forty more days of winter. February was the month of purification in which the errant souls circulated before ascending the Milky Way. The Church established the 2nd of February as *the Purification of the Virgin Mary,* thus combining the Greek *Anthisteria* and the Roman *Lupercalia* and *Parentalia.* This day was also known as *Chandlers,* the name being derived from the candles carried in Church processions. These candle-lit processions originated in Greek, Roman and Egyptian antiquity, where they were used to guide the souls of the dead to their old homes. Torch-light also figured in the cult rites of Demeter and Persephone. The next forty day cycle began with *Ash Wednesday,* the start of the Lenten period.

Progressively, each day of the year was dedicated to a specific saint with certain functions. Within the carnival season, the 22nd of January was dedicated to St. Vincent, who now took over Dionysus' domain as patron of the vintners. In France, the conversion of St. Paul fell on the 25th of January. In the Midlle Ages, St. Paul was the patron saint of cord makers, and on this day great carnival fires were kindled to burn the remainder of the hemp plants after the long fibres used in making ropes had been removed. The people would dance around these purifying winter fires, no doubt inhaling the smoke from the burning plants. The 1st of February honoured St. Brigitte, who, according to Christian legend, helped the Virgin Mary deliver the newborn Jesus. She was associated with fertility and childbirth. The cow was her animal and she was thought to promote lactation. St. Blaise, the master of the winds, was honoured on the 3rd of February. Like the bear who released the souls of the dead whenever he passed wind, St. Blaise controlled the travels of these souls as they rode the winds up the Milky Way. He also adopted the powers of Odin, the Teutonic god of the winds. St. Agatha's day was the 5th of February. She was the protectress of nursing mothers and women. In Spain, she was represented as an old woman capturing winter in her sack. A witch-like figure, she was said to live in cemeteries and was associated with cats and death. The saints assumed the many powers of the old gods: promotion of fertility, the growth and revival of vegitation, protection at childbirth. They were even associated with the animal incarnations of the old divinities.

The only aspect of carnival that Christianity can legitimately lay claim to, is the term "Carnival" itself, and even that has been a constant source of debate. Some etymologists contend that the word is derived from the ship on wheels, "carrus navalis", central to so many of the antique and medieval rites.

Most of the linguistic evidence suggests that the word "Carnival" is after all a Christian invention, stemming from the Latin base, "carne–vale", or "carnelevare"; "carne" meaning "of the flesh", and "vale" meaning "farewell", or "levare" meaning "to take away". Carnival referred to the period of license which preceded the forty days of fasting and abstinence culminating in the resurrection of Christ on *Easter Sunday*.

Further adjustments of the liturgical calendar in the early 9th century fixed the start of Lent forty days before Easter, which fell after the first full moon of spring. *Mardi Gras, Shrove Tuesday* and *Fasnacht* climaxed the three final days of carnality before *Ash Wednesday*.

The impression given by the Popes was that the Church had magnanimously granted the privileged feedoms of the fat days and therefore had the authority to curb their excesses and limit their celebration. So convinced was the Church that carnival was part of its own tradition that when the 17th century

Protestant Reformation abolished the hardships of Lent, the Christian reformers naively insisted that there was no further need for the sinful carnival.

After centuries of vain ecclesiastical prohibitions the Church had little choice but to tolerate the popular festival, even though it continued to characterize carnival as the most unfortunate and reprehensible event on the face of the earth. The war on carnival and its excesses was eventually turned over to city councils, most of which were dominated by the Church.

The Popes consoled themselves, philosophically rationalizing that Christianity was after all the religion of the urbane, the cultivated and the civilized. If the primitive customs persisted, particularly in the rural regions, it was clearly because the ignorant peasants lacked the light of reason.

But the traditions of carnival survived in the hearts of the rural pagans, who, because they lived close to nature, understood the magic cult rites of their ancestors. The heavy-handed christianizing, moralizing and allegorizing of their ancient customs had little effect. The demons of antiquity continued to thrive in the popular imagination, and the rural folklore glorified them. These demons inherited the legacy of the ancient gods which embodied the mythical concepts that blended paganism, popular regional beliefs and superstitions into folklore.

Cult to Custom

THE FOLKLORE OF CARNIVAL—AN ANCIENT HERITAGE

Each corner of Europe had its own version of legendary adventures and fabled encounters with supernatural beings. Tales of death and burials, ghosts and devils, wood spirits, dwarfs and giants, magic places and sorcerers, witches and sacred animals, provided each carnival with its own unique tradition and an incredibly colourful cast of characters.

The Death of the King of Folly

The king, of course, is the star of carnival who acts out the passion of death and resurrection. He is at the same time hero and villain who brings joyful anarchy and the folly of a world turned on its head. In some regions he is very regal and appropriately dignified with a royal court, in others he takes on a playful, burlesque character.

In old Spain, he was chosen as "King of the Roosters". In prudish England where carnival season was reduced to a family celebration, he was "Lord of Misrule" or "King of the Bean". Whoever in the family received the slice of cake containing the bean reigned from *Halloween* to *Shrove Tuesday*. In parts of Italy and France he still appears in carnival processions as a straw effigy. The Italian term "Paggliaccio" stems from the word "paglia" = straw; and in France, the fool is called "Pallaise", derived from the word "paille" = straw. In the north of

France and in Flemish Belgium, he takes on gigantic proportions as a descendant of the folkloric "Gargantua", or the giants of the Druid cults. In the Tyrolean Alps, he is a newborn baby represented by a mischevious doll known as "Naz" who squirts water at the crowds.

Since Carnival is the culprit under whose magic spell we commit all the madness and debauchery, at the end of the wild celebrations he stands accused of his sins. A long list of his crimes is read at farcical tribunals which judge his misdeeds and condemn him to death. In parts of Italy where the honoured role was played by a living man, Carnival read his last will and testament leaving everything he possessed to the new year. He was then laid in a coffin while great crowds of tearful mourners lamented his passing. Throughout Europe his straw effigy was executed by firing squades, hung, drowned, buried or ceremoniously burned on funeral pyres.

Ironically enough, it was not always an effigy that suffered the tragic fate of King Carnival. In 1393, Charles VI of France went up in smoke when his leafy "Wild Man of the Woods" costume was accidentally touched off by the careless Duke of Orleans. In the early 16th century, Alexander de Medici gave his life during carnival in Florence, no doubt with the result that his countrymen could breath more easily.

Many carnival animals sacred to the old

The "Bœuf Gras" Procession in Paris   11
1856

gods met the same end. These poor creatures, condemned as scapegoats or divine incarnations, were sacrificed and eaten at carnival feasts. The cock, a carnivalesque animal in both France and Spain, was sacrificed in a variety of cruel games. In one such game, the unfortunate bird was tied to a stake with a long string while revelers stoned him to death. Indo-European folklore considered the rooster a symbol of life who battled death and evil spirits, and these sadistic games put his mythical powers to the test.

In Cologne, a bizarre carnival game, still practiced at the end of the 15th century, involved five blind men and a pig. A large pen mounted on a cart was pulled through the streets of the city. Inside this pen, a pig was tied to a stake, and the blind men armed with clubs wearing protective armour had to beat the animal to death.

In northern Europe, the bones that remained after the carnival pig had been eaten were saved along with rooster feathers to be ploughed into the fields during spring sowing to ensure a bountiful harvest and to protect the crops.

Another animal king who gave his life for carnival was the bull. The Druids offered him in their winter sacrifices to the sun god Bellen. The Greek Menaides tore him to pieces as the young Dionysus. In France, the bull was fattened, his horns decorated with laurel garlands, ribbons and flowers–he was the "Bœuf Gras" of carnival. After a triumphant Mardi Gras procession during which the bull carried yet another king on his back, the "Roi de Bœuf", the huge animal was slaughtered and then eaten. The "Bœuf Gras" inspired the fantastic carnival character "Tarasque", a huge bull-like creature made of cloth and cardboard who was played by several men hidden inside.

In many rural celebrations, especially in remote mountain regions, a dramatic hunt was re-enacted, the object of which was a dreaded vegitation demon who appeared in the form of a bear, acted by a man. Bear and hunters represented winter and spring in a ritual confrontation of the forces of nature. Another character who was ritually hunted and killed as a representative of winter was "The Wild Man of the Woods"; it was in this costume that the unfortunate Charles VI of France met his untimely end.

These carnival dramas are still acted out in France, Germany, the Tyrolean Alps and parts of Eastern Europe. Cats, too, often suffered the fate of the animal scapegoats because of their association with sorcerers and witches. The Druids had burned them in their giant wicker cages along with cattle and men. Vestiges of this custom survived in Europe for many centuries. Cats were burned on *Mardi Gras* in the Vosges mountains of Eastern France. Louis XIV burned a sack of live cats in his carnival fires at Versailles. In the late 19th century, cat and rabbit fur was used to make elaborate bat costumes for one of the allegorical floats in Nice's Mardi Gras parade.

Witches and Fools

The carnival season, especially between Christmas and the Epiphany, is also witching time. It is a time when supernatural creatures, ghosts, phantoms and sorcerers lurk about.

In Italy, for example, one of these figures is the "Befana" whose name is a corruption of the word Epiphany. The Church councils of the 6th century disapproved of this figure of the "Old Woman" and tried to incorporate her into the calendar as St. Agatha. During carnival, her effigies were hung in windows and small pastry figurines in the shape of the witch were thrown about in the streets. According to christianized legend, the "Befana" had two sons, one Carnival, the other Lent.

In southern Germany and Austria, ugly witches, the "Perchta" and the "Holda" led the so-called *Tanz der Schemen* or *Schemenlaufen,* a grotesque procession of phantoms, ghosts and demons. Those representing the spring were beautifully dressed and masked whereas those representing winter and evil spirits were hideous.

In the Bavarian Alps, witches danced and lept over great Fasnacht fires. The Italians and Germans used to burn straw witches in their carnival fires. At the end of the 18th century, the Swiss were still driving witches, or "Posterli", from their villages. In various parts of Europe, noisy processions of dis- 40 sonant horns, clattering pots and pans, bells and loud shouting expelled spirits and witches in much the same way as the classical Greeks drove out the "Keres" at the end of their *Anthisteria*.

Macabre processions of ghosts could and still can be found throughout European carnivals. Many of these phantom processions were led by the "Hariloking" of Anglo-Norman legends. The "Harlequin", as he came to be known, was king of a diabolical army of dead souls which terrified and delighted carnival crowds. "Harlequin's" fame and popularity spread throughout European folklore making him a universal figure of carnival. The devilish "Arlecchino" inspired the Italian Comedia dell'Arte. He gave birth to a host of carnivalesque characters, the French "Pierrot" and the humpbacked "Pulchinelle" who imitated the cry of the chicken, the Russian "Petrushka" who inspired Stravinsky. In Germany he was the oafish "Hans Wurst", in Spain "Don Christobal". His colourful patched costume was adopted by the "Charivari" who performed indecent farces and poked fun at their audiences. "Harlequin", a descendant of an ancient god, is part man, part supernatural being who can command the elements. He is both quick and clumsy, sharp witted and stupid, playing the dual role of devil and fool.

In the Middle Ages, the fool was regarded with superstition and fear. He was considered as a supernatural creature who had mysterious powers and links to other worlds and dimensions. In the disorder and confusion he generated, it was difficult to tell where his oafish ignorance ended and a cunning joke began. Always the clever joker and malicious prankster, he transformed the meaningful into nonsense, and vice versa. He dressed in a three-coloured costume, red, green and yellow–the fool's colours. When he put on his horned fool's cap, all were equal.

According to ancient legend, the fool was born under the same horoscope as the king who was his equal. The fool's magic number 11 symbolized that equality, two ones side by side. In the Medieval court he enjoyed the unique privilege of telling the king truths that could not be uttered by any other mortals. The fool would often speak in verse, spitefully making fun of everything and everybody with impunity. He could be crude and derisive, ridiculing the king's court, revealing their intrigues, making them laugh and blush, exposing their weaknesses, their lust, their hypocrisy. His buffoonery both amused and annoyed. He was continually getting into scrapes, and up until a hundred years ago, Basel's fool, the "Uli", was annually dunked into the Rhine. Many carnivals of the Rhine Valley open each year in the 11th minute of the 11th hour of the 11th day of the 11th month–the fool's magic moment.

The Dance of the Elements

Carnival is a propitious time for magic. Medieval alchemists waited for the special moment, in which the stellar configurations coincided with certain lunar or solar cycles, to catalyze the transmutation of the elements. Carnival is that moment and its magic performed by the fool or the priest magician transforms both social and natural elements.

The smoke from the purifying carnival fires revealed omens for the coming agricultural year. Bones from traditional year-end meals were saved along with feathers from roosters. These were mixed with ashes from the sacred fires, and then strewn over the fields to protect the crops from disease and pests. The rounds or farandols–chains of dancers encircling these fires–had special powers. Jump dances where legs have to be lifted high mimicing the growth of plant life are still performed in Germany and Austria.

The magic stomping dance, as old as man himself, is danced to this day in Flemish Belgium. Its asymmetrical stomping rhythm, danced to an ancient trance-inducing drum cadence, generates an incredible primal energy that hammers at the frozen earth waking up the spring and driving out the demons of winter. In the Alpine regions of Germany, Switzerland and Austria, dancers wear huge bells that are sounded in unison as the performers execute a special step to ring in the new cycle.

Carnival rituals are full of magic instruments, special gestures and criesthat have specific powers. In Belgium and in certain parts of the Alps, a symbolic broom is used to sweep out winter. In French and German carnivals, inflated pork bladders, said to contain the souls of the dead, are attached to the ends of sticks and used to beat members of the opposite sex. Like the ancient Roman "Februa" of the "Luperci", blows from these magic wands stimulate reproductive powers.

In many carnivals today, these sacred instruments have degenerated into plastic clubs, but their ritual function remains unchanged. Gangs of youths playfully, and sometimes not so playfully, beat young girls or each other. Their battles are vestiges of ritual competitions re-enacting the cosmic struggle of winter and spring. At one time such battles were a key element of many rural carnival games, but, like the old Roman celebrations, they were eventually suppressed because of the violence.

Mock fights still survive in the rather tame form of "Orange Battles" found in Italy, Switzerland and Belgium. In Nice, once the site of wild pitched battles where dangerous plaster confetti, clumps of rock-hard dried dough, egg shells filled with sand, cinders or pepper and the volleys of rotten fruit left scores of casualties, the custom has been refined to what is called, *La Bataille des Fleurs,* the "Battle of Flowers". Young girls

The last masked ball in Rome 1872   12

riding on lavishly decorated floats throw yellow mimosas, a traditional carnival flower, to crowds lining the streets.

Laurel, which was forbidden by the Church councils of the Middle Ages, thyme and rosmary were also typical for carnival, and during the carnival season twigs and branches of these plants were hung from the windows to keep away the evil spirits.

Many foods eaten during carnival season were also thought to have magical powers. The ancients believed that eating the flesh of animals sacred to the gods, such as pigs, cocks, goats and bulls, would impart mythical powers. Special cakes in the shape of these animals were baked. Rich greasy foods were served with flatulants, beans or peas to facilitate the release of the dead souls. Another typical carnival custom that has survived to this day is the throwing of flour. In Basel, Switzerland, a special soup made with burnt flour is served for Fasnacht. In other European cities, pancakes or crêpes are still traditionally eaten. The very act of excessive gluttonous consumption was part of the magic ritual promoting the germination of seeds in the field, the conception of children, good fortune and prosperity in the coming year.

The Eroticism and Grandeur of Carnival

The erotic elements of the ancient orgiastic fertility rites have all but vanished from the European celebrations. The sacred marriages have disappeared, even in rural areas.

13
The Carnival procession
in Nobility Hall, St. Petersburg
1883

German peasants no longer bind fruit trees in ritual matrimony so that their orchards will be fruitful. As the idyllic pastoral way of life faded, many of its traditions also died out. There was no further need to stimulate the regenerative forces of nature because nature had been conquered and its secrets made known to everyone. The king of carnival still has his queen, but she is usually played by a man. Even the German custom of marrying on carnival Sunday has gone. Traces of the lust-inducing bawdiness characteristic of the old rites persist in carnival games and street theatres but in no

44

way compare to the indecent farces of the medieval festivals.

Centuries of moralistic repression at the hands of the popes, bishops and state authorities, changing economic and social conditions, tamed the freer wanton spirit of licentiousness that was the heart of carnival in antiquity. The sensual festivals of Renaissance Europe described by Rabalais and Montaigne faded.

European celebrations in the 17th and 18th centuries began to change into what eventually became modern carnival. These transformations took place in an era of opulent post Renaissance decadence. Louis XIV of France held court for luxuriantly costumed mythological gods and goddesses who, under the protection of disguise, participated in the extravagant "Bœuf Gras" processions through the streets of Paris.

This "Bœuf Gras" was followed by huge floats of papier mâché animals. The bourgeoisie would throw potatoes boiled in oil and occasionally containing gold coins into the crowds. Lavish masked balls were held at Versailles, Fontainebleau and the Opera.

In his "Travels in Italy", Goethe described the mammoth proportions of Rome's carnival in the 18th century. Man's instincts of liberty and fantasy were given free reign. Hundreds of theatrical presentations were staged in squares and parks throughout the city. With most of the violence and debauchery under control, the accent of carnival became artistic expression, and no expense was spared. Plays and poetic fables replaced obscene farces. Huge processions of allegorical floats wound through the streets of Rome, and young and old alike participated in them. Gone were the violent fights, the public nudity and immorality that had once characterized the carnival celebrations. The Colliseum hosted giant spectacles with tens of thousands of musicians, dancers and singers.

The carnival in Venice that had so enchanted Byron with its opulant splendour and immense wealth, glorified carnival into a monumental expression of artistic genius that was celebrated for six months out of the year.

By the 18th century, carnival was being celebrated from India to Imperial Russia to the colonial Americas, enjoying its golden age of universal popularity. But the age of revolutions changed all that, radically inverting the social order in many parts of the world. Carnival and revolution have never mixed well, the one too serious, the other too frivolous to see that their goals are identical.

In many cities carnival died, never to be resurrected. In rural areas the cult rites were slowly suffocated by the endless industrial revolution, accomplishing in just a few short centuries what the Church had failed to do in twenty.

Custom to Commerce

CARNIVAL IN THE SQUARES OF THE OLD WORLD

The European carnivals that survived the grand festivals of the Renaissance and the Bell Epoque, did so largely due to the cities and towns dedicated to their traditions and determined to preserve them in some form or other. In an age of social turmoil, revolution and war, the urban centres could no longer tolerate even ritual anarchy. The 19th century saw a reformation of carnival, christalizing the content and the structure of the celebration, too often at the expense of its tradition and spontaneity. The old agrarian cult magic had lost its power for the urban man, but the need for ritual was still in his soul. Carnival committees sprang up all over the continent endeavouring to provide the old rituals with new forms. These committees recognized the need for ritual but saw it mainly as a need for distraction and entertainment. The result of their reformation is modern carnival.

The success of their organizing efforts varied just as it had in the Middle Ages under the Church reforms. The urban areas suffered the most, and many of the large carnivals disappeared completely. The ones that survived either became spectator events or large popular festivals with little of the cult ritual remaining. These large, very popular European celebrations are found in Germany's Cologne, Mainz and Munich, in Italy's Viareggio and in France's carnival in Nice. Smaller, more traditional celebrations were less effected by this trend towards grand

commercial spectacle and can still be found throughout Europe, and although their rituals are often mixed with recent adaptations, the ancient elements of cult are still very strong. The carnivals of Dunkirk and Limoux in France, Rottweil in Germany, Basel and Lucerne in Switzerland, and Binche and Malmedy in Belgium are examples of such celebrations.

The purest surviving traditions have been the ones blessed with geographical isolation. Europe's mountain regions are full of village carnivals that have remained virtually unchanged for centuries. Their cult rituals are performed in earnest and the traditions are handed down from generation to generation. In the French Pyrenees, the Swiss, Bavarian, Italian and Tyrolean Alps, as well as in many East European villages, the people still cling to their ancient customs.

European carnival is again flourishing, and each year celebrations grow as more and more people participate in them. Zurich's carnival, for example, banned and dormant since the Protestant Reformation, is now enjoying a revival.

The Carnival of Cologne

Cologne hosts Germany's and possibly Europe's biggest and most lavish carnival. An ancient outpost of the Roman Empire, Cologne's tradition was influenced by 46

Carnival in Cologne
1854

14

Teutonic, Roman and Greek cults. After centuries of church and state prohibitions and the strict policies of occupying armies, much of the ritual has disappeared from the carnival of Cologne. During the French occupation masking was prohibited outright. When the French were replaced by the Prussians in the early 19th century, fines were levied against masqueraders. Later, registration of masks was required during the celebrations. Eventually, people stopped wearing masks altogether, and today they are rarely seen.

The early carnival celebrations were very individualistic, and many groups organized small private carnivals. Guilds formed their own processions, each headed by their own "Jecken" or fool. The various professions designed costumes symbolic of their guilds and performed dances. The barrel makers' guild staged colourful hoop dances, the smiths danced their sabre dances, and the butchers paraded animals. Rivalries between these various groups often deteriorated into violence. The Church organized pious diversions to distract the people from the raucous street festivals.

In 1823, Cologne formed its first carnival committee to unify these varied and often competing elements into one big carnival. In this era of domestic nostalgia, old traditions were renewed or transformed. Many of the characters who now identify Cologne's carnival emerged from its romanticized past. The traditional king or hero of carnival, the "König Lustig", is the prince, dressed in red robes with ermine trim and plumed crown. Instead of a sceptor, he carries a huge wooden ratchet, called the "Pritsche". He is accompanied by the "Bauer" and the "Jungfrau"–the Peasant and the Maiden. The "Jungfrau" symbolizes the glory of Cologne as a city of the Roman Empire that has never surrendered its virgin purity to any foreign power, and the stout "Bauer", ever ready to defend her virgin honour, has been the symbol of Cologne ever since the days of the Holy Roman Empire. This trio represents modern carnival in Cologne. They are accompanied by a military guard–the "Rote Funken", meaning red sparks, and dancing camp followers–the "Tanzmariechen". Both of these characters have their origin in the Prussian occupation of the early 19th century. Another character that has survived the committees' reformation is the "Jecken", the fool who announced carnival for the various guilds.

Today carnival in Cologne opens on the fool's magic moment, the 11th of November, at 11 minutes past 11, when the "Elferrat", or Council of Eleven, that constitutes the committee declares the start of the carnival season. Only a few masqueraders come out for the ceremony in the old market square.

During the next four months, hundreds of meetings, balls and reunions are held to pick the three most honoured representatives of carnival, to choose and practice the songs for the various song competitions and to hear the humorous "Bütte Recitations". The term "Bütte" refers to the wash tub podium symbolic of the ritual spring cleaning which used to be customary, and it is on this podium that the "Bütte Recitations" are held. The "Bütte Recitations", which are often spiteful and satyrical, focus mainly on the political controversies, scandals, gossip, rumours and mishaps that have spiced the local scene in the past year. Some of the recitations and particularly the selections and competitions for the carnival songs are broadcast as television specials. This festive pre-carnival season culminates on the Thursday before Mardi Gras when the so-called *Weiberfasnacht* or women's carnival bursts onto the streets of the city. This is a tradition which began in the 1880's as a feminist protest against the exclusively male domination of carnival. Today it signals the official opening of the street celebrations.

At 11 past 11 on Thursday morning the mayor arrives at the old market square shouting to the crowds, "Kölle alaaf", which means "Hail Cologne". He then hands the keys of the city over to the prince 48 of carnival and his two partners who will rule for the next five days. The "Rote Funken" guards present their arms and rears in a parody of the military parades called "Wibbln".

To the delight of the spectators and especially her partner, the charming "Tanzmariechen" does her traditional acrobatic dance. Before the 1930's, the role of the "Tanzmariechen" was played by a man. The pristine "Jungfrau", whose honour the brave "Bauer" is ever ready to defend, is still played by a man today. This traditional male role was grudgingly relinquished to a woman for two years when Hitler's Reich forbade any member of the virile master race to disgrace himself in women's clothes. One of the reasons still offered for not allowing a real virgin to play the part, is the exhaustingly heavy schedual of appearances the coveted role demands.

After the opening ceremony, the emancipated women of Cologne take to the streets. The first target of their affections is the police upon whom they rain wet lipstick kisses. The whole city now belongs to the women. Rumours fly that adultery committed during carnival is not recognized by the courts. Masquerading women joined by hopeful suiters turn the old market area into a mad playground with processions of drunken Cologners stumbling from tavern to tavern singing and swaying arm in arm yelling, "Kölle alaaf", drinking Kölsch after Kölsch, Kölsch being the local beer, while the women plant wet kisses on every male in sight.

Relief from the drunken street carnival can be found at countless masquerade balls sponsored by neighbourhood societies, student and professional organizations. At many of the larger affairs the regal trio makes guest appearances and watches the entertainment.

Another tradition of Cologne's carnival are the theatre presentations. The city has managed to preserve the spirit of the old street theatres so popular in medievil carnivals. Puppet theatres, nearly an extinct art form except in children's parks, have been revived and now provide the comic relief of the old street farces satirizing the local and national scene. Today's theatre presentations, considerably tame by comparison, have been moved off the streets, and now represent an important element of Cologne's carnival.

After the *Weiberfasnacht*, the streets are relatively calm for the next two days. Before the war, a ghost parade was held during this period. People dressed in long white sheets, painted their faces white, carried green lanterns that cast a deathly pallor on their faces and held a phantom torch-light procession through the streets of the city. But after the war the custom was never revived.

Today the many larish masquerade balls provide most of the evening diversions of Cologne's carnival. The more formal the entertainment, the more likely it is that the regal trio will make its appearance. Their prestigious presence is always eagerly a-waited, especially by the promoters of these functions, who rely on them to provide the climax for their commercial success.

To be chosen as one of the three symbols of Cologne's celebration is an expensive honour that is bought rather than bestowed. The investment can, however, become very profitable since the many television appearances increase personal prestige and assure advertising contracts and commercial endorsements. In this way traditions often get commercialized or pushed out in behind-the-scenes manœuvres of promoters and carnival committees.

One such competing tradition which nearly succumbed to committee pressures is the popular *Schull- und Veedels-Zög*, a procession held on Sunday in the old section of Cologne. This very animated and spontaneous street parade is made up of small floats, marching bands, masqueraders and dancers organized by local neighbourhood groups, schools, churches and small businesses. It is an intimate carnival held for and among friends. The procession makes its way through narrow crowded streets jammed with children, friends and neighbours. Family groups all dressed in the same carnival costumes parade along with the floats. People hang from their windows with inverted umbrellas yelling to their friends on the floats to throw them flowers and sweets. Cologners proud of their own local celebrations, will boast that the Schull- und Veedels-Zög is the city's true carnival.

But Sunday is only a small prelude to the un-rivaled spectacle staged by the city and the "Elferrat" the next day. *Rosenmontag,* or Rose Monday, is the parade that has made Cologne's carnival the most extravagantly generous celebration in Europe. Miles of giant floats, decorated cars and wagons, the many neighbourhood floats, marching bands, dancers, the honour guards–both "Rote Funken" and "Blaue Funken", carnival bands playing off key music with battered instruments, the "König Lustig", "Bauer" and "Jungfrau" riding their luxurious float–all parade for hours through the packed streets of Cologne throwing out tons of sweets, bouquets of flowers, large and small, bottles of Eau de Cologne and Schnaps and many special gifts for friends they see along the way. No one leaves the Rosenmontag parade empty-handed or disappointed. On Monday night there are more masked balls, more appearances of the now famous trio, more humorous presentations and more dancing and drinking in the streets till the early hours of the morning.

On Tuesday, a final ball organized by the "Elferrat" is held for the "Jecken" or fools. This is followed on Ash Wednesday by the traditional *Heringsschmaus,* a sumptuous feast of hering and other fish.

50

Morgenstreich in Basel 1873

The Fasnacht of Basel

Carnival is over, burned and buried. Ash Wednesday has come and gone. The period of excess and wanton license is over. Further up the Rhine, just across the border in Switzerland, Basel is beginning to bubble, final touches are being added to costumes. On the streets, muffled strains of fife music and drum rolls drift in the air. While the rest of Europe is penitently atoning its sins, Basel prepares for its magic hour, *Morgenstreich*. The Baslers wait until the Monday after Ash Wednesday when everyone else has bidden farewell to the pleasures of the flesh to begin their Fasnacht. Some suggest that the fiercely independent Baslers were so furious about the Church's incessant prohibitions and limitations on their Fasnacht that to show their contempt they decided to double their sins and not only to celebrate carnival but to do so during Lent as well.

In the Middle Ages Basel was a pious religious centre, and therefore the Baslers had to fight that much harder to preserve their traditions. In the 16th century, the Church banned all masking. Nevertheless, carnival continued as a spontaneous roudy affair. Youths would dress as ghosts, skeletons and witches, roam through the city luring people out of their houses, smearing tar on them, then powdering them with ashes and dunking them into fountains. Various guilds would hold parades. As in Cologne, hoop dances and sabre dances were performed, often ending in bloody battles and even death. Violence was rampant. Outside Basel great bonfires were lit around which the Baslers battled with sticks. In spite of Church prohibitions the people wore masks, and the city council recognized that the mask had certain privileges and cautioned shopkeepers to lock up their shops as no protection could be offered. The butchers were a favourite target of thieving masqueraders, sausages being a traditional carnival food. Attempts to control or at least to separate the wilder celebrations from the city led to the creation of special carnival days for women and for children.

In the 18th and 19th centuries, Basel began to adopt many of the customs that so distinguish its Fasnacht today. The fantastic masks that instantly identify Basel were introduced in the 19th century. The fife and drum came to Basel from France. Torchlights were used to light the processions for the drummers, later replaced by beautifully painted lanterns, also from France.

In the early 18th century, in spite of Church protests and condemnation the "Vogel Gryff" or griffin as this tradition is known in Basel, was incorporated into the Fasnacht tradition. The introduction of this custom reflects the notorious disdain Baslers hold for whatever is not of Basel. The residents of "Groß-Basel", the old part of the city on the west bank of the Rhine, still swear to this day that the "Vogel Gryff" has nothing whatsoever to do with their Fasnacht as this ritual is held in "Klein-Basel" (Little Basel), which was never considered to be part of the city. The tradition, however, is older than either part of Basel and predates the Roman influence in this area. For many it is the opening of carnival.

About a month before Fasnacht begins in "Groß-Basel", a raft floats down the Rhine carrying a wild man or forest demon dressed in a leafy costume wearing a terrifying brass mask and carrying an entire pine tree complete with roots. Drummers, flag bearers and four fools known as "Uli" accompany him. He comes ashore on the east bank in front of the old Guild house where he is joined by two other mythological creatures, the "Vogel Gryff" and a lion. Each of the trio does a special dance for the officials assembled, they then move on to the house of another dignitary and repeat the ritual. To show their scorn for the snobbish "Groß-Baslers" the trio always keeps its back to the west bank of the Rhine. The closest they will come to "Groß-Basel" is the middle of the old bridge. This procession is followed by a large crowd. Children dart out of the crowd trying to snatch small apples attached to the wild man's costume while he tries to sweep them away with his pine tree. This game can get quite rough. In the old days when the lion's role was much more aggres-

52

sive, unlucky victims swept off their feet by the wild man were thrown into the nearest fountain by the lion.

For the "Groß-Baslers", Fasnacht starts just before dawn on the Monday after Ash Wednesday. This tradition began as a playful mockery of the military. One early morning reveille, the soldiers of the garrison called out for muster found themselves being followed by a troop of masqueraders accompanied by the fife and drum. Commemorating this morning, thousands of Baslers from all corners of the city crowd into the big market place and overflow into the surrounding small streets and alleys. In the cold sober silence, the air is thick with anticipation as Basel waits for the magic moment when the church bell strikes four and the alchemy of the *Morgenstreich* begins.

On the first bell all the street lights go out, and the entire city is plunged into erie darkness, on the fourth bell the drum rolls begin, and thousands of fifes join in. Suddenly, the darkness is pierced by one, then two, then hundreds of the beautifully painted lanterns that each group or clique has been secretly working on all year. Now everything begins to move to the stuttering coffee grinder cadence of the Basler drummers. For the next three days and nights this entrancing cadence continues as hundreds of cliques wind their way through the city. They pause at taverns and restaurants, they drink, they eat the traditional "Mehlsuppe" made with burnt flour and then go out again to the sound of the fife and drum.

On Monday afternoon, the cliques appear in their full regalia, displaying the themes painted on their lanterns. Drum majors in their huge masks, fifers and drummers dressed in their costumes and masks, complementing the cliques' chosen theme, lead processions of floats from which mimosas, confetti and oranges are thrown. Satyrical rhymes known as "Zeedel" printed on long, coloured pieces of paper are handed out. In the evening, groups of players wander from tavern to tavern, giving yet another form of humorous recitation, called the "Schnitzelbangg", in which the satyrical verses are punctuated with comic images from a story board. Local personalities and events of the past year are satirized in verse form, written in the "Baseldiitsch" dialect, even some of the Baslers themselves have trouble following. The clever play on words is often so closely tied to local events that even a brief absence from the city can leave a Basler puzzled at the punch line. The spirit of irony and satire is the real heart of Basel's Fasnacht. The humour of both the "Zeedel" rhymes and the "Schnitzelbangg" was originally very bawdy and the tradition nearly died out. The custom was revived, by the Fasnacht committee which succeeded in preserving this unique art form by offering prizes for compositions with the sharpest wit and sense of irony.

53

So fond are the Baslers of their mocking spirit that they take this custom one step further onto a personal level in what is known as "Intrigieren", meaning intruiging. A hapless victim, often a pretty girl or someone the intruiger knows, will be confronted by an anonymous mask, perhaps an "Alte Tante", the nasty old aunt, who knows too much. This is a classical Basler Fasnacht character, also called the "Fasnachtsfrau". In a muffled voice the old gossip will wag her tongue, joking and teasing, trying to fluster and embarrass her victim. This "Intrigieren" may be suggestive but never vulgar or vicious. Once the old hag's victim is disarmed, the mask melts into the crowd. This confrontation can also be an overture from a secret admirer too shy to make his intentions known otherwise. Often a victim will be surrounded by more than one intruiger, one holding her, another stuffing confetti down her back and whispering the intruigues in her ear.

On Tuesday, the "Guggemuusig" bands come out and the fife and drum recede into the background. These huge brass bands were introduced in the 19th century. They play off-key refrains that seem to deteriorate into complete cacophony only to be rescued at the last moment by the real musicians in the band. Before Fasnacht, classified adds in the Basel newspapers advertise for musicians capable of carrying a tune. When a "Guggemuusig" band passes, everything vibrates to the brass dissonance of its beat up, dented instruments, many of which are converted and adapted with long hoses and extra horns, giving them a comic motley appearance.

On Wednesday, everyone comes out, the "Guggemuusig" bands, the fife and drum, wagons throwing oranges and flowers to the crowds. This is the grand finale that lasts late into the night. There is more "Schnitzelbängge" and more "Intrigieren"; phantom bands march the streets even after everyone else has gone home, and fife and drum wander through the narrow alleys which echo their enchanted refrain.

These hard-core cult initiates eventually converge on the small Andreas Platz, the heart of Fasnacht for many Baslers. Here at dawn the celebrations are unofficially closed with a football match and an egg fight. Later that morning many Baslers will accompany their drunken friends from neighbouring Alsace to the train station. Officially, however, Fasnacht ends with what is known as the "Kehruus" the sweeping out, and in some places the digging out from under the tons of confetti that cover the city. No sooner have the last flakes of confetti been swept off the streets, than the cliques, drum rolls still echoing in their heads, meet again to plan next year's Fasnacht. And thus the tradition lives on, and the Baslers are very proud and protective of this tradition. Young people who congregate on the Andreas Platz to   54 make their own music, banging on cans and cowbells, are met with boos and protests for violating tradition. Individuals not belonging to any particular clique and who venture out in costumes and masks that do not conform to the strict code are also reproached and derided. But protest is in the Baslers' blood. The Fasnacht committee, created to preserve the old traditions, is usually fending off some kind of protest or other.

Basel's traditions are hardly pure in origin. The march played by most cliques is "Arabie", an English grenadier's march. The "Waggis", one of the most popular clique costumes, was adopted under protest from neighbouring French Alsace. The "Charivari" and the "Blätzlibajas" costumes of multi-coloured tattered patches are descendants of the Harlequin tradition which was spread throughout Europe by the Italian Commedia dell'arte. Basel's crossroad position on the Rhine leaves it open to all forms of influence, and these continue to invade the tradition it so closely guards.

The Schleicherlaufen of Telfs

Isolation is often the key to cultural integrity. Europe's remote mountain retreats have, for centuries, preserved many authentic elements of pagan fertility rites no longer found in urban carnival tradition. Not even the remotest villages, however, were able to escape the domineering influence of the Church. At the beginning of the 18th century, the so-called "Vierzigstündige Gebet", prayer lasting for forty hours, was introduced to keep the inhabitants of the Tyrolean villages from celebrating Fasnacht. And for centuries, the *Schemenlaufen* of Imst, a grotesque Fasnacht procession of phantoms, ghosts and demons, was declared immoral and sinful. It was considered dangerous for unborn children, and pregnant women were advised not to cast even one glance at the grotesque "Schemen".

In spite of this, western Austria's Tyrolean Alps have managed to preserve a rich folklore that predates Roman and even Germanic influences. Many of these rites and some of the characters, such as the "Perchten" of the Tyrolean carnivals of Imst and Nassereith are unique to this area. They are ugly witches who lead the *Schemenlaufen*. Other characters, such as the "Scheller" with their huge cowbells, and the "Roller" with their smaller bells are found throughout the Alps. In Telfs, the main characters are known as "Schleicher", and the Fasnacht of this village is named after them.

The first reliable source mentioning the *Schleicherlaufen* are court records from the year 1768. According to them, a couple of Fasnacht merrymakers were sentenced to bread and water behind bars for two days because of their indecent behaviour during the "Maskererlaufen", a parade of masks.

The Schemenlaufen on the Market Square of Imst   16
Karl von Lutterotti, about 1845

The village priest refused to receive Easter confession from those who had participated in the Fasnacht celebrations. He also rained reproaches on them in a special sermon and sprinkled them with holy water.

The term *Schleicherlaufen* refers to the very quiet, graceful slinking step made by the "Schleicher", the incarnations of spring, as they creep up on winter. These "Schleicher" wear magnificent hats, some of which are up to one meter tall, weighing over eight kilos. The hats, usually allegorical tableaus of idyllic pastoral life, are made of carved wood, dried flowers, nuts, corn, sheaves of wheat, even stuffed animals. Underneath the hat there is a wire screen mask with the face of a young person painted on it.

Each "Schleicher" makes his own hat. The costumes are magnificent and are made of coloured silk and velvet. A huge bell attached to a wide belt is worn around the waist, and when the "Schleicher" move ("Schleichen"), they are not allowed to let the bell ring. In his right hand each "Schleicher" holds a stick stacked with about twenty baked prezels–symbols of the sun. In his left hand he holds a folded white linen handkerchief. In the old cult ritual, a wet cloth was used to strike the partner of the "Schleicher" in a symbolic gesture of fertilization.

This partner, known as the "Roller", can   56

still be found in the carnivals of Imst and Nassereith. He has, however, disappeared from the celebrations of Telfs. In Telfs, it is customary for forty "Schleicher" to form a circle around yet another traditional group consisting of the "Tuxer" and the "Tuxerin", the "Senner" and the "Sennerin", the "Goaßer", the "Wirt" and the "Kellnerin". The "Tuxer" represents the rich land holding farmer, the "Tuxerin" his wife. The "Senner" and the "Sennerin" are the dairyman and dairymaid who work on the high alpine pastures during the summer. The "Goaßer" represents a goat herder, the "Wirt" an innkeeper and the "Kellnerin" a serving girl.

As soon as the magic circle is closed, the "Goaßer" sounds his horn, known as the "Alphorn" made from a special root. This is the signal for the "Schleicher" who now begin their unique slow step. The forty giant bells sound their low, resonant ring that vibrates the earth and echoes in the village and the mountains calling for spring and for a fertile season of growth. An 18th century proverb says that when Telfs celebrates its carnival, the corn grows taller.

Like so many traditional carnivals, the "Schleicherlaufen" of Telfs begins at dawn. A group including a baker, an innkeeper, a chimney sweep and a peasant carrying a golden sun attached to a long pole, form a procession. This procession stops at every intersection of the village to recite a prayer beseaching the sun to smile on their carnival and to send sunshine in plenty, but not to overdo it so that no one will suffer sun stroke. The Telfers cannot remember any carnival that has had to be cancelled because of bad weather.

Later in the morning, the so-called "Wilden", or wild men, appear. These grotesque, creatures are believed to be the descendants of the ancient mythical giants supposed to have once inhabited the Kochental valley behind Telfs. With their terrifying masks, these incarnations of winter are the adversaries of the "Schleicher" in the elemental struggle of the seasonal spirits. The wild men also make their own costumes. Both young and old must climb to an altitude of 2000 meters to pick the green lichen from which their shaggy costumes are made—avalanches making it an extremely dangerous venture at this time of year. Their impressive masks are made by local wood-carvers who carve the mask out of a single piece of wood and then fit it exactly to the face of the person who will be wearing it.

After the wild men have made their appearance, Telfs' oldest carnival ritual is acted out in a meadow behind the town. Hunters dressed in skins disappear into the forest at the edge of the meadow to hunt bears. Their hunt will give them the bears' power. An oriental horde representing the barbarian invaders of Europe waits in the meadow for the hunters to appear with their quarrey. As soon as the hunters and the bears reach the meadow the wild horde stages a savage attack capturing the bears. The group then triumphantly returns to the village where a large parade is beginning to form up.

This parade consists of various traditional and less traditional groups, bands, floats, a gypsy wagon, a circus group with a menagerie of animals, horsemen representing the four seasons and heralds announcing the opening of carnival. The wild men are responsible for maintaining order—a fact that would have been inconceivable in the last century. For in the 18th and 19th centuries, the wild men were true to their name. They roamed the streets of Telfs completely drunk and riotous, attacking anyone who crossed their path.

The procession is followed by a very traditional character, the "Laternenträger", or lantern bearer. This harliquinesque fool in his huge five pointed hat covered with rows of corn kernels swings a giant lantern symbolizing the light of spring. His role is to search for carnival in the darkness of winter. While dancing lightly, swinging his lantern, he makes room for the "Schleicher".

The "Schleicher" now form a circle and dance the first round to a successful Fasnacht. The magic gong sounds and the procession moves on to repeat the ritual at the next square. The last round danced in front of the church is dedicated to the "Schleicher" who have died since the last carnival.

This is followed by an old Tyrolean custom, the so-called "Labera". The community and its leaders are made fun of by a mock tribunal which judges and condemns archetypal characters. This delights the spectators who recognize themselves and their neighbours in this burlesque trial, and it is considered almost an honour to be included in the "Labera".

In the midst of all this, a wagon pulled by the "Laninger" appears carrying the "Naz", a doll representing the carnival baby. Six weeks before Fasnacht, when the carnival preperations begin, the "Naz" is officially "unearthed" in a ritual act. It now sprays the people with jets of water squirting from its mouth. This is an act of ritual fertilization which can be found in many traditional carnivals. The "Laninger" is a group representing medieval nomads who, similar to the gypsies, lived by their wits, usually on the wrong side of the law, rejecting the traditional way of life of the community. In the back of their wagon, one of the "Laninger", the so-called "Zanger", pokes his head out from under the canopy, laughing and mocking the crowds. He sticks his tongue out at the spectators to show them that the "Laninger" have the last laugh and that they are the real fools, not only for watching this nonsense but also for the serious lives they lead. At the end of Fasnacht, the "Laninger" and the various groups tearfully bury the "Naz" who will be "unearthed" again in five years time for the next *Schleicherlaufen*. Nearly all the elements of Telfs' carnival have a function which goes beyond entertainment. The allegorical floats, the humorous parodies, the hunt and the dance all serve the community either by performing an ancient agrarian cult ritual that still has vital importance to the prosperity of the town, or by serving to air grievances and cementing differences, thus bringing the members of the community closer together. The tradition of this Fasnacht has survived because the people needed it and because they understood its power. They are proud of this tradition because they live it and because it is handed down from father to son. Even though the women are excluded entirely from the ritual, nearly the whole community participates directly or indirectly in the preparations and the celebrations themselves. Further adding to the power and mystique of these truly communal rituals, is the irregularity of the celebrations. The years they are held are anxiously anticipated and carefully prepared for long in advance.

Mardi Gras in Binche

The Flemish town of Binche in Belgium celebrates a carnival that has also managed to preserve elements of ancient cult rite and community ritual. In the carnival of Binche, it is the "Gille" who performs the sacred magic that transforms nature. The "Gille" is an evolution of the archetype "Polichinelle" character with his two hump deformities, made of straw. It is he who manipulates the occult instruments and dances the ancient steps that renew and revive.

Local history has influenced his evolution and even obscured his origins, suggesting that he was born at a mid 16th century festival held by Marie, widow of Louis II of Hungary, the regent of the Low Countries, to commemorate the Spanish conquest of Peru. Belgium was under Spanish rule at the time and rumours about the fabulous Inca empire began to circulate. The great plumed headdress of the Incas became associated with the "Gille's" own plumes and thus legend was spawned. One of the largest societies of "Gilles" is called "Inca", and its members insist that the "Gilles" are descendants of the Inca.

Carnival in Binche opens on the 22nd of November, St. Cecil's Day. The preparations begin on the succeeding Sundays. Balls, meeting rehearsals, reunions of carnival societies and "Soumonce", or convocations are held. February 2nd is Chandlers, and from this day on masking is authorized on Saturdays, Sundays and Mondays.

February 2nd is the day when ghosts and spirits are released to circulate among the living. On the Monday before, the *Jour Gras*, or fat days, these ghosts come out in force. In Binche this night is called the "Trouille de Nouille", "Trouille" meaning fear of the unsavoury character, and "Nouille" meaning noodle, refering to the long tube through which the maskers drink so as not to be recognized. On this night, all manner of ghosts, witches and "old women" roam the streets, bursting into homes, getting into mischief and making sarcastic remarks to passers by in disguised voices. They can usually be appeased with drinks, and the drinking which takes place during the carnival of Binche is legendary, rivaled only by Cologne's celebrations.

On Sunday morning, masqueraders appear as "Mam'zeles" in long elegant dresses but very masculine faces. The women participate in the carnival of Binche as spectators only. These male "Mam'zeles" are accompanied by organ grinders. In the afternoon other masqueraders join in, and brass bands and drummers provide the music. Large processions wind through the streets of the town dancing to the cadence of the drummers. They dance the ancient "Basse Dance" or stomping dance. As night falls they dance from tavern to tavern drinking more and more. This is Binche's night of masked chaos and drunken revelry.

Monday is Children's day, most everyone spends it recovering from the excesses of Sunday and preparing for *Mardi Gras.*

At dawn on Tuesday morning, the ritual begins, and the "Gilles" are already up and dressing. A special "Bourreur" or stuffer comes to stuff the "Gilles'" humps with straw. Tradition dictates that only a "Bourreur" can do this work not just any member of the "Gille's" familiy. In every house the champagne bottles are on the table, for on this day the "Gilles" drink only champagne. The bells, the bonnet and the clogs are put on. The "Gille" listens intently to each drummer that passes, nervously waiting for the familiar cadence of his own society. For the "Gille" cannot move without the drummer who comes to fetch him on this morning and who will escort him to his doorstep twenty-four hours later. The drummer goes from house to house collecting the "Gilles", and at each stop, toasts of champagne are offered. As the "Gilles" dance through the streets, the town begins to wake up. People gather on the sidewalks to watch the excitement. When a "Gille" sees a friend in the crowd he waves and throws the "Ramon" to him. This sceptor-like symbolic broom is used ritually to sweep out winter. The "Ramon" used to be a real broom made of twigs, and the "Gilles" would gently strike their friends with these brooms to bring them luck and prosperity. Today the "Ramon" is thrown and then returned, but the gesture remains the same.

Now masked, the "Gilles" dance toward the town hall where they are received by the mayor and claim the city. Later in the afternoon they appear again, wearing their great

The Mardi Gras in Binche 17
1891

plumed hats, one and a half meters tall and weighing two kilos. The front of the hat is decorated with an agricultural symbol of golden sheaves of wheat and oats. The "Ramon" has been replaced by a wicker basket full of oranges, and during the afternoon parade, the "Gilles" rain oranges down on the crowds. Other societies, the "Pierrots", the "Little Gilles", the "Harlequins", "Sailors", "Peasants" and "Princes of the Orient" join the huge procession funneling into the big town square where they dance the great rounds.

At night they return again. Through the dark streets they come, stopping only to dance around burning red flares symbolizing the sacred carnival fires, the then moving again toward the town square. Slowly they gather like ancient pagan tribes to dance around the Bengal fires. When the last society has reached the square they all dance their final rounds under the spectacular fireworks which cascade over their heads. The crowds disperse, the tourists go home, and yet the "Gilles" dance on. Mardi Gras has been celebrated, Lent has begun. At midnight, the police should really confiscate all drumsticks but the drummers still hammer out their timeless cadence. On empty narrow streets, the different societies meet and pass through one another dancing to their own rhythm, never losing a beat, each completely entranced by its own cadence. As if mesmerized by the ancient rhythm, the "Gilles" dance their magic step, alternately stopping and then starting again. Oscillating between dimensions they transcend into the supernatural state where the cosmic forces are released, transforming winter into spring.

La Bataille des Fleurs in Nice

On the other end of the spectrum, far from the occult and the cosmic, are the mundane carnivals that have completely lost touch with their roots and have become lavish show business productions for the entertainment of paying tourists. Not only have all the cult rituals been purged, but the spontaneous participation of the public has also been structured out of these staged celebrations in which the participants are hired to play in front of passive spectators. Whereas in most carnivals the tourist is a tolerated byproduct of the celebration, in these spectacles he has become their reason for being.

Europe's most tourist orientated, internationally known carnival is hosted by Nice on the French Riviera. However, Nice's carnival has roots as old as any other European celebrations. First founded as a Greek outpost and later under Roman domination, this area adopted the many cult rituals of these two cultures.

From the Renaissance to the end of the Belle Époque this coastline was the fashionable winter playground of the European royalty and aristocracy. Even before revolution changed Nice's complexion from aristocratic to bourgeois, the resort was tourist orientated and its carnival became an attraction rather than a ritual. Records show that Nice's carnival was already on the royal tourist calendar in the 13th century when Charles II of Anjou enjoyed the celebrations in 1294.

Class consciousness has always been acute in Nice and even the equalizing spirit of carnival has failed to overcome this prejudice. In the Middle Ages separate organizations were formed to control each of the carnival celebrations according to class: nobles, merchants, artisans and labourers. City ordinances allowed citizens to attend balls below or above their station in life but only in full masquerade. This was, however, more a concession to the roving instincts of the aristocracy than any respect for the principals of equality sacred to carnival. In the 18th century this liberty was further restricted, permitting dancing with members of another class only if masked. After each dance the masks had to be removed, and the partners discreetly seperated to join the company of their own class.

In 1848 the French revolution effectively banned all masking, later tolerating it as in Cologne but only with stringent precautions. Masks had to be registered, a special tax was levied, and slowly they disappeared from the celebrations. The only aspect of Nice's carnival that seemed to resist government control was its roudy street festivities. The notorious battles of plaster confetti, beans, eggs, and even more dangerous missiles continued to the end of the 19th century. These battles were observed by the aristocracy from safe balconies and terraces. In 1860 one such observer was Maria, the Grand Dutchess of Imperial Russia. With more and more royal heads of state wintering in Nice, the city's efforts to control its carnival increased.

In 1873 a carnival committee was founded, whose members were counts, dukes, barons and bankers. The rather exclusive profile of this organizing committee set the tone for Nice's carnival, and it has retained it to this day. The committee's first communiqué fixed the dates, the route of the "Corso" or parade and introduced a couple of novelties: stands to which admission would be charged and from which the parade could be observed, and prizes for the most attractive float. The committee promised spectacular lighting displays along the route of the "Corso", allowed a small ceremony at which the traditional effigy of Mardi Gras could be burned, repeated the ban on battles with eggs, flour and fruit and forbade any religious or political allusions in the floats or the masquerades. The famous *Bataille des Fleurs,* or battle of flowers, was introduced in 1877 as a distraction from the excesses of the street battles and as an attraction for respectable tourists. The committee even inaugurated special "pleasure trains" to bring these refined spectators to their show from the coastal towns between Marseille and the Italian border.

The early casualties of this organizing were the traditional customs of carnival. The classic character "Polichinelle" was replaced by "His Majesty Carnival", the giant papier mâché king, who is still the most important figure of Nice's celebrations. The "Paillassou", a straw dummy thrown in the air by masqueraders holding a sheet, was another part of the popular games and farandoles or dances that also disappeared. Many carnival games, street farces and characters such as the mischievous "Charivari" were banned because of their roudiness and mocking satire. Even the "Moccoletti", an ancient Roman custom, eventually disappeared. The "Moccoletti", little candles whose flames, representing the souls of the dead, were the object of a carnival game. Using handkerchiefs, masqueraders would try to extinguish each others candles while protecting their own. An extinguished flame meant a soul had been released. But this game also faded under the bright lights that decorated the route of the "Corso".

The disappearance of old folkloric customs transformed the Nice carnival into a lifeless and humourless show for the elité. Shortly after the inceptions of the committee, the thematic orientation of the corsos was also fixed: Two competing floats–one a nostalgic, romantic, allegorical presentation–the other an imaginative representation of the demonic and supernatural world, were chosen as finalists. The "Ratapignàta" float symbolizing the hellish underworld with devils and fantastic bat costumes made of cat fur was the overwhelming popular choice. The committee, favouring the elegant allegorical float more in keeping with its dignified image, rejected the popular favourite and nearly touched off a riot. After this incident the themes of the corsos remained strictly in the realm of fantasy.

Today the fantastic floats are the saving grace of Nice's bourgeois carnival. The giant, grotesque monsters that awe and fascinate the crowds in the grandstands are a marvel of ingenuity and creative imagination.

But Nice's reputation was not made by the artists who spend months conceiving, constructing and animating these wonders. The carnival of this Azure Coast resort is renown for its flowers. The famous *Bataille des Fleurs*, battle of flowers, is a grand seafront parade of beautiful floats luxuriantly decorated with cut flowers. Pretty young girls dressed in elegant gowns or as bathing beauties toss bouquets of flowers to the admiring crowds. An illuminated nocturnal version of this parade again features the girls in more revealing skimpy cabaret style costumes. After the *Bataille des Fleurs* completes its rounds in front of the fashionable hotels and casinos, crowds descend on the floats to carry off the exotic floral decorations. The more sophisticated spectators retire to exclusive "veglioni" or masquerade balls where the most popular disguise seems to be formal evening wear. On the festive night of Mardi Gras, Nice's surviving cult tradition, the burning of "His Majesty Carnival", is climaxed by a spectacular fireworks display.

Il Corso di Viareggio

Further down the coast, on Italy's Tuscan Riviera, another seafront show carnival of collosal proportions is celebrated in the old port of Viareggio. During the Belle Époque 64

19
The Temptations of Satan
Viareggio, 1911

Viareggio was also a retreat for the wealthy, though the much smaller town never became as fashionable as Nice. Both inherited Rome's carnival traditions, especially the "Corso" that evolved into the huge parades and giant floats seen today. But here the comparison ends.

Viareggio was never dominated by a humourless bourgeois elite, and the class antagonism between the relatively poor port area and the fashionable beach resort was always vital. The early carnivals were wild and spontaneous. Masqueraders danced through the streets going from house to house, often impudently invading the formal gatherings of the bourgeoisie. The police would have to intervene, ejecting masks not in keeping with good taste. Street celebrations were often violent. The early floats were mostly decorated carriages that masqueraders rode around in.

In 1874, following the European trend to control and structure the raucous street celebrations, Viareggio's leading citizens decided to form their own carnival committee. They more or less organized the first modest

"Corsos" that paraded through the old city centre. The early themes allegorized the romantic nostalgia of the epoch and the naive positivism toward the promises of the industrial revolution. Floats represented the marvels of the new era of science and technology. The tradition of poking fun at authority, inherited from the Roman *Saturnalia,* expressed the class antagonism that existed in Viareggio. The newly formed committee was barraged by complaints from their influential colleagues who recognized themselves as the butt of mocking jokes and satyrical presentations. In spite of these complaints the spirit of satire prevailed and was increasingly incorporated into the floats. When the committee moved the route of the parades to the wide open spaces along the fashionable shore line the "Corso" mushroomed. Each year the floats grew bigger in proportion and more spectacular in conception.

For centuries Tuscany had been an artistic centre providing the European courts with their marble sculptures. The transition from stone to papier mâché was a natural one for Viareggio's artisans. Local folklore, politics and personalities provided the themes for their ever growing creations. Soon their sculptures reached mammoth proportions, two to three stories high. The artists known as "Maghi" (magicians), eventually outgrew the petty local intrigues. The proportions of their incredible creations were big enough to take on the world. No inept leader or corrupt official, no corporate scandal, no national or international issue escapes their biting satire. Each year thousands come to Viareggio to see who the "Maghi" have chosen to mercilessly caricaturize and what new scandal will be the target of their acid humour. They come to laugh with the "Maghi".

They also come to dance the "Tarantella", to drink and to sing in the streets. The other side of Viareggio's carnival, the popular side, is celebrated in the neighbourhoods. The three weeks before *Martedi Grasso* are punctuated by grand "Corsos", and local neighbourhoods take turns hosting their own street carnivals. These small celebrations full of life and sponteneity draw large crowds. There is music to please all tastes, from traditional to punk, and the narrow streets are packed with dancing masqueraders, the "Arlecchinio", the "Pulcinella" and the "Burlamacco", Viareggio's own adaption of the Harliquinesque character. Small floats sponsored by neighbourhood groups parade through the crowds. Children are everywhere, beating on each other with plastic clubs and throwing confetti into the gaping mouths of the unwary. The community spirit is alive and animated, everyone is in the streets echoing the words of Viareggio's carnival song, "Carnevale é il vecchio, che la vita ci Ridá!" (Carnival is the old fool who gives us life!)

66

Slums and Salons

CARNIVAL IN THE STREETS OF THE NEW WORLD

For all its splendour, its pageantry traditionalism and ever growing popularity, carnival in Europe has with notable exceptions lost most of its vitality. The frenzied delirium, sensuality and elements of primal madness that have been the core of ancient cults since time immemorial have nearly all been purged. European carnival has been tamed and caged, let out once a year on a short leash under careful supervision.

Democracy, industrial and social revolution, and the rise of the middle class have effectively erased Europe's visible class structure. The classical tensions between master and servant, between rich and poor–tensions that carnival so deftly inverted and relieved–have been neutralized. The conquest of nature, the emancipation of women, the sexual revolution have evaporated the licentious sexuality of the Bacchanalian rites. Twenty centuries of structured religions and civil authority have civilized the wild unruly gods of antiquity. In these twenty centuries the gods have been restrained many times only to resurface again doubly strong. When the Roman legions exported their tired pantheon to pagan Europe they saw it flourish in the fertile soil of Indo-European tradition. When the colonizing Christians brought their religion to the new world, they unwittingly introduced the same ancient gods who for centuries had been masquerading as Christian saints.

The Spanish, the French, the Dutch, the English and the Portugese with their armies and missionaries were generally well received by the noble savages of the New World. The white man was openly and generously welcomed. The red man was repaid for his hospitality with carnage and bondage. To console him in his misery and to make him believe that his fate was the will of God, the zealous missionaries offered him Christianity. To humour the conquerors the Indians adopted this faith but they were much less receptive to enslavement. Their noble temperament would not bow to servitude. Many chose death, others died of the white man's diseases or were exterminated. But the new empire had to be worked so slaves were imported from West Africa. Thus another cultural heritage from yet another part of the world was mixed with christianized tradition.

In Central and South America the Spaniards were driven by dreams of gold–El Dorado. They found their gold in the form of priceless ritual relics of the ancient pre-Columbian civilization. The treasures made from the sweat of the gods were melted down and shipped back to Spain. They also found an incredibly rich cultural heritage.

In Mexico, the Conquistadors found the descendants of the Mayas and Aztecs. These cultures performed cult rituals to the powerful deities of their ancestors. Like the Egyptians, these civilizations divided their calendars into lunar cycles. And like the ancients of the Eastern Mediterranean they also had five superfluous days between their old and new year. These days were called "Nemontemi" and were considered useless.

The "Nemontemi" fell between January and February. During these days, the Mayas of the Yucatán made clay images of the devil and exorcized him from their villages. The devil was believed to have poisoned the old year. To drive him out, the clay devil was confronted with an image of the god who embodied the power of the new year.

At winter solstice, the Aztecs made images of the god "Huitzilopochtl" out of dough and seeds from special plants, kneaded with the blood of children. The image was ritually killed by a priest who acted the part of the god "Quetzalcoatl". After the image had been stabbed with a dart, the priest cut it into pieces that were given to every male in the community. These sacramental rituals which even included incest were remarkably similar to many pagan year-end fertility rites practiced in the old world.

When the Christians introduced their own year-end celebrations, the pre-Columbian gods and the pre-Christian gods blended easily. The festivals to the spirits of the new year, rites of exorcism, dances to the corn gods and the rain spirits were adapted to the religion of the Conquistadors. The Indian gods assumed dual roles and Christian names to placate the missionaries. Carnival that corresponded so well to their own cosmology, with its masks, numerous spirits, dances and sacrifices resurrected the gods of the old world into the new.

The history of carnival in Spanish South and Central America bore a great resemblance to the European experience. In the 17th and 18th centuries, the Church and civil authorities tried to gain control of the pagan idolatry and the popular excesses of the celebration. The heritage of violence from the Conquistadors mixed with the old ritual battles turned the *Entrudo,* the Spanish and Portugese version of the carnival procession, into wild and often bloody street games. By the 19th century carnival in the Spanish Empire had reached its apogee. The tradition was firmly established and made respectable. Many of the old customs celebrated in the colonies of the neglected Empire survived in far purer form than they had in Spain.

Carnestolado Fiesta in Mexico

In Mexico or New Spain, huge parades were held even surpassing the splendour of many European pageants. "Corsos" with floats and processions of Indians in tribal dress with plumed headdresses and fantastic masks paraded through the capital. Allegorical floats with politically satirical themes that would never have been tolerated in the Mother Country amused the upper classes.

20
Quetzalcoatl
Illustration from a 16th century
manuscript, Mexico

The grandeur of European society was re-created for the wealthy at lavish masquerade balls. The lower classes held street festivities. They dressed in ragged clothes and even indiscreet costumes, a rarity in the morally rigid Catholic society. Carnival celebrations were not confined to the capital and became a kind of national holiday. To this day towns and villages all over Mexico hold their own carnival festival or *Carnestolado Fiesta*.

In the state of Sinaloa on the Pacific coast, the resort city of Mazatlán hosts one of Central America's largest carnivals. Like most resort areas that hold such celebrations, the old carnival traditions have nearly all faded. Mazatlán's festival once opened with the old custom of burning "Bad Humour", a sad-faced straw effigy that represented the ill humour of the whole community and was destroyed to ensure a joyous celebration.

Mazatlán has a bullring and during carnival the bullfight with all its inherent elements of ritual sacrifice draws tremendous crowds. Thousands flock to this seacoast town from the surrounding communities to participate in the celebration. They come to see "Momo", the King of carnival, and "La Reina del Carnaval". Unlike Europe, the central figure of carnival in the Americas is the Queen. During the festival, beauty queens from all over Mexico come to Mazatlán to be part of the Carnival Queen's regal entourage. To become Queen of Mazatlán's celebration, local candidates enter a city-wide competition to raise money which goes towards paying for the festival. The local beauty who raises the highest contribution from the community is crowned at a gala surrounded by Miss Mexico and a host of other Misses imported for the occasion. Even beauty queens from California are invited each year. The children of Mazatlán have their own Queen of Carnival. No function, no gala, masked ball, theatrical presentation or reception is complete withouth them. The only relief from these ever-smiling, ever-waving mechanical dolls is the "Rey Feo", or ugly king of carnival, who attends many of the official ceremonies adding a burlesque touch to the almost compulsive latin fascination of the Mexicans with their Queens.
The grand climax of official carnival is a huge parade of floats, one for each of the attending beauties. Allegorical floats, and even some political themes intersperse the beauty pageant.

The street carnival is much more animated. Hundreds of "Mariachi" bands that flock to Mazatlán for the festivities provide music for singers and dancers. For a few pesos they play requests or accompany revelers who sing their hearts out to appreciative crowds. Stages are set up in various squares throughout the city where bands play for people dancing in the streets. Children roam around throwing confetti and breaking "Cascarones", dried egg shells with bits of coloured paper inside, over their victims' heads. Young unmarried girls promenade with their watchful chaperones, matronly aunts or grandmothers who make sure there are no breaches of the strict moral code. The tone of this carnival celebration is decidedly conservative, a trend that seems to hold wherever Spanish influence has prevailed.

Mas in Trinidad

Wherever the Spaniards lost their colonies through neglect or war, particularly in places where the West African culture was introduced by the European colonists' black slave trade, the evolution of carnival took a much wilder, more liberal turn. In the two hundred years of carnival in Trinidad, a

Carnival in Port of Spain   21
Trinidad, 1888

Caribbean island off the coast of Venezuela, this festival has become one of the world's most colourful and artistically spectacular celebrations.

Columbus discovered Trinidad at the end of the 15th century, and although the Spaniards took possession of the island and made it their colony, Spain neglected it for nearly a hundred years. Decades would pass without a single Spanish ship entering the harbour, and by the mid 16th century the Indian population had been almost completely decimated by slavery and disease. Black slaves had to be imported to work the plantations, and Spain began to take a more active interest in its possession.

But it was the French rather than the Spanish who brought carnival to Trinidad. In the mid 18th century, French planters who were trying to escape from the slave uprisings on Haiti, Martinique and other French possessions, took refuge on Trinidad. The Spanish encouraged this immigration by offering land grants. By the late 18th century, immigrants were pouring in with their slaves and their customs.

The early carnivals were strictly for the planters and were celebrated from Chistmas to Ash Wednesday. The season was highlighted by fashionable masked balls where the whites dressed as field slaves, "Negué Jadin" (from the French, "négre jardin" = garden negro). They blackened their faces and danced to the rhythm of African drums. Slaves were excluded except to give special performances for the entertainment of their masters.

When slavery was abolished in 1834, the freed blacks celebrated their own carnival, adding their rich West African traditions to the European customs. From the cultures of Guinea, Dahomey, the Yoruba, the Ibo of Nigeria and the Ashanti of Ghana came many rituals and dances: the "Bamboula", "Ghouba" and "Kalinda" stick dances. Cult figures from their West African folklore joined the carnival masqueraders. Some of these like the "Papa Bois" (father of the woods), a protector of animals who could assume the shape of any forest creature, resembled the Roman "Faunus" and the European "Wild Men of the Woods". Others, like the "Moco Jumbie", a menacing figure on stilts, "Shango", a devil spirit, and "Mama Deleau", the water mother, were adopted from the pantheon of African deities, spirits who are still worshiped today in *voodoo* cult rituals. The former slaves blackened their faces to resemble the "Marrons", their pure black ancestors. The blackening of the face was a custom associated with the devil both in West African and Indo-European tradition. The Romans also blackened their faces during their winter celebrations.

The freed blacks had an acute sense of humour and mockery. They would dress in white masks and parody their former masters. To commemorate their bondage, *Canboulay* processions were made a part of carnival. The word "Canboulay" is of French origin and refers to "cannes brulées", meaning burning cane. *Canboulay* became the central theme of black carnival symbolizing the violence inflicted on slaves. If a plantation caught fire slaves were rounded up from the neighbouring plantations and driven with whips to fight the fires. The former slaves covered themselves with black varnish and paraded through the streets of Port of Spain carrying chains and sticks yelling, singing and cracking whips, mimicking their former masters and parodying their slavery. The sticks they carried were used in "Kalinda" dances of African origin, a popular dance and ritual battle. These choreographed stick fights often became violent.

After the emancipation of the slaves, the white man's carnival began to deteriorate. The French withdrew from the wild street festivities and held their own refined masked balls in their luxurious mansions. The street rabble, nudity and fighting outraged the white elité. The many European immigrants and indentured servants from India, China and the Middle East stayed away as well. For them the celebration had become dangerously out of control.

The British, who took over the colony at the end of the 18th century, did their best to abolish carnival altogether, but with little success. They found the drum offensive to their sensitive ears. However, for the blacks the drum was not only an essential part of their carnival dances but also central to many of their cult rituals. The mask was also banned and military force had to be employed on several occasions to enforce restrictions. But the emancipated slaves refused to abandon their carnival that for them had already become a symbol of their freedom and had taken on aspects of a mass cult ritual. When in 1883 the over-zealous police attacked the masqueraders trying to enforce a ban on Sunday masking because it was considered to be a desecration of the Lord's Day, the blacks fought back with their "Kalinda" sticks. This triggered off the *Canboulay* riots which were to change the face of carnival in Trinidad.

The following year no *Canboulay* procession took place–it had been banned. Carnival now began on Monday morning at six with the *Jouvay* or "jour ouvert", open day. The carrying of sticks was prohibited except for the "Pierrot" character adopted from the French tradition, and he had to get a special permit to perform the "Kalinda" stick fights.

Towards the turn of the century the street celebrations became civilized again and the upper class began to join in. Masked bands began to form, first as a parody of the British military who were there to maintain order. Then music was added, mocking and competing with the string bands and orchestras of the whites. The blacks used very rudimen-

tary instruments, drums and hollow bamboo stalks of various length, that were hit with sticks and blown through to give varying pitched sounds. These were known as "Bamboo Tamboo Music Bands" and they accompanied the African folksongs. In 1838 the Port of Spain Gazette described this tradition as a "disgusting and indecent African custom of carrying a stuffed figure of a woman around on a pole, which was followed by hundreds of negroes yelling out a savage Guinea song". These savage African folksongs became calypso. First sung in French patois and later in English, they were often bawdy, mocking the refined ladies of the island, protesting social conditions, and satirizing the ruling elite. Public singing of profane songs was banned, so the music moved into tents. Bands would play, humorous skits from African folklore and satirical pantomimes were performed, calypso songs were sung.

The calypso tents became showcases of African culture, and now are the greatest source of popular music in the Caribbean. The "Bamboo Tamboo Music Bands", which the British also tried to abolish, eventually evolved into Trinidad's other claim to musical fame, the "Steel Pan Bands". Searching for a new musical instrument, carnival revelers began beating on large metal cans. The ingenious Trinidadians turned the surplus oil drums left over from the second world war into sophisticated musical instruments–and another art form was born of carnival.

Eventually the Sunday that had been desecrated by the masqueraders and had ended in the *Canboulay* riots was returned to carnival. Now *Dimanche Gras,* as it is known, perpetuates the traditions of the old tents by staging "Limbo" and "Kalinda" dances, "Ol'Mas" farces and satirical mime presentations ("Mas" means mask), King and Queen of Carnival competions, the calypso song competitions and, when the Pan Bands are not striking for more money or boycotting, the "Panorama" or "Steel Band" competitions.

The King and Queen competitions show the most spectacular imaginative fantasy costume creations to be seen in any carnival. Some of these huge allegorical centrepieces are so big they can hardly be moved without the wheels and rollers attached to them. Yet according to the rules of the King and Queen competition each competitor must move across the stage unassisted and be able to dance in costume. Some are marvels of structural engineering 10 meters wide and weighing 150 pounds. However, the designs have been known to fail in mid performance crashing down around the exhausted masquerader's head. Costumes, no matter how spectacular, are disqualified if their design fails. The King and Queen costumes are but a small preview of what follows on the next two days.

Jouvay begins the actual street masquerading and dancing. In the old days classical costumes would come out on *Jouvay.* The "Pulchinellos" and Indians were very popular. Many pirates with wooden pistols appeared, characters inspired by local legends, for the Caribbean was full of pirates in colonial days. There were also many skeletons, "Papa Bois" characters and stick fighting "Pierrots", "Boba", an old woman similar the the European "Befana" character also came out for *Jouvay.* The "Jab Molassi" or molasses devil, smeared with molasses mixed with soot, would go around menacing bystanders and demanding money. Today a tame version of this demon appears with his arms and hands smeared with mud or sticky chocolate. Many of the traditional costumes have disappeared. Today most people wear ragged clothes for morning Jouvay and dance through the streets following two-tiered "Steel Pan Band" carts pushed along on wheels. Children's "Mas" or "Kiddy Carnival" begins later in the morning. In the afternoon a preliminary warm-up for the big day is held in the town road marches.

Tuesday is the climax and is called *The Last Lap*–"Last lap we go make bassa bassa". "Bassa bassa" is a Yoruba expression meaning wanton destruction. On this day the giant parades of "Mas Bands" jump up and dance across the vast stage, past the reviewing stands in the final competition for band

74

of the year. Bands, some over a thousand strong, illustrate the allegorical theme whose centrepieces are the fabulous King and Queen costumes. Thousands pass the judges' stands, jumping up, dancing wildly to the music of the "Steel Pan Bands". The costumes vibrate in the afternoon sun, as the "Mas" players put their last ounce of strength into their last lap. Some do not make it and surrender to sweet exhaustion, collapsing on the enormous stage, and have to be helped off by friends.

The bands continue on into town, where more exhausted masqueraders walk out of their costumes as if they were shedding a skin. Children instantly recover these empty relics, keeping them alive until their own strength gives out. Late into the night, crowds of masqueraders too tired to jump up simply shuffle along behind the rolling pan carts keeping a rhythmic beat with their wooden clogs. Lovers in a back to belly embrace shuffle the final leg of the last lap following the carts back to the pan yards and "Mas" camps.

Mardi Gras and Rara in Haiti

While Columbus was sailing around the Caribbean in search of India, he discovered and claimed for Spain one on the most mysterious and enchanting islands of the Western Hemisphere, the island of Hispaniola.

This paradise was inhabited by Arawak Indians who believed the island they called Haiti to be the cradle of the sun and the moon. The Spaniards soon turned it into a hell on earth, decimating the Indian population and importing slaves to replace them. In Catholic Spain the enslavement of heathens was forbidden. This seemingly humanitarian restriction was quickly circumvented by the bishops who permitted the slave trade only under the condition that the Africans be christianized.

By the end of the 17th century Haiti had become a rich Spanish possession. The French then took over and within a hundred years made it the richest most exploited colony of the New World. They occupied the western half of the island and turned Cap Français into a town of luxury, refinement and fabulous wealth—the Paris of the West Indies. By the end of the 18th century so many slaves had been imported to exploit Haiti for the French Empire that there were 17 black men for each white. With the odds clearly in their favour, the slaves followed the example of North America, their freedom-loving neighbour, and revolted.

This, however, is where the first two independent nations of the new world parted company. The world turned its back on the impudent slave revolt. Without effective leadership Haiti floundered and became the victim of countless international intrigues. At the beginning of the 20th century, the

"Big Brother" to the north intervened, administering the island for the Haitians. The people resisted this occupation, and in the 1930's the Americans were eventually obliged to leave. They left, taking with them the country's entire gold reserve as compensation for the administrative services rendered by them to the ungrateful Haitians. The richest island in the Western Hemisphere became the poorest–but at least it had gained its freedom.

The slaves who had fought for that freedom, paying an awesome price to keep it, came from West Africa–from Guinea, Nigeria and Dahomey. They came to Haiti, bringing with them their pantheon of gods, "Jegba", "Ogun" and "Shango". After a while these gods aquired Christian names, but when Haiti gained independence, "Voodoo"–a Dahomian word meaning spirit or god–began to flourish.

Voodoo is a cult bound to the soil and to the elements of nature. Drums, dances and songs honour and summon divinities who take possession of the dancers. Dance and trance open the door to a dimension where spirits and man can communicate. These *Voodoo* gods or "Laos" live on an island beneath the sea from where they surface to help the people overcome illness and spiritual problems, to advise and console them but also to punish them. Propitiatory ceremonies are performed to the earth, sky, water and to the seasons. Symbols of the natural environment are used to influence the cosmic forces. The spirits of dead ancestors play a vital role in these rituals. The dances and sacrifices offered to these spirits closely resemble the ritual and mystic cosmologies of the ancient world. Here again the gods of the old world surface to appear in the new.

An annual Haitian celebration containing many elements of carnival is the *Rara*. "Rara" is a Yoruba word meaning loud and noisy. In the colonial era, torch-lit processions of dancers dressed in costumes would follow bands similar to the "Bamboo Tamboo Bands" of Trinidad. Shuffling their feet in a rhythmic accompaniment to the music, the Haitian slaves would dance from house to house collecting money and food in a brightly decorated basket attached to a long pole. These festivals lasted from Ash Wednesday to Easter. Accounts of the *Rara* festivals from the mid 19th century describe them as huge processions of shuffling dancers and overt sexual exhibitionism in which everyone participated. They were headed by a "Roi", or King, dressed in a regal red robe and wearing a great headdress. Large families and unexpected childbirths were attributed to the loud and joyous *Rara* festivals. Today the *Rara* is still celebrated throughout Haiti.

Mardi Gras of French origin has become an extension preceding the spontaneous exhuberance of the *Rara*. In Port au Prince,

Carnival in Haiti   22
1883

decorated stands are constructed and
painted with the naive works of art so typical of Haiti. It takes hours for the huge procession of floats, dancers and masqueraders
to form before starting through the streets.
Many traditional costumes no longer seen in
Trinidads' carnival are still very much alive
in Haiti. The "Marrons", for example, represent the African ancestors who fled the
French slave camps to form the revolt that
was to liberate Haiti, are smeared with black
sooty varnish and wear loin cloths, others
wearing cardboard crowns masquerade as
African kings.

77   The Arawak Indian costumes, honouring
the extinct native tribe, are the most spectacular masquerades. Bizarre pirates painted
black with huge lips and carrying wooden
pistols menace the crowds and ask for
money. The "Loup Garous", devils from
African folklore, strange animals, bats, and
even real boar's head masks follow the
floats. Here and there beautiful faces
painted according to West African tribal
rituals peer out of the crowd. "Les Bœufs"
–the bulls–a traditional character of French
carnival, have become horned harlequins
with long tails who crack bull whips along
the entire parade route.
Loudspeakers blare "Merengue" music
while elaborately decorated floats pass carrying beautiful mulatas who wave to the
crowds. Most of the floats are sponsored by

local businesses who take this opportunity of advertising their products. These are ridden by upper class, fair skinned blacks, the ruling class of Haiti.

There are no political or satirical floats to speak of because there are no politics in Haiti. Rare individual masqueraders, however, do express very mild protest against the abysmal poverty and social conditions. Many groups and dancers wave Haitian flags and banners proclaiming, "Vive la difference", "Vive Duvalier". Jean Claude Duvalier, the young president for life, son of the dreaded "Papa Doc", affectionately called "Bébé Doc" in private conversation among trusted friends, watches the procession from behind the iron fence of the Royal palace. Flanked by machine gunners and body guards, he approaches the fence to shake hands with his people and to throw "Vive Claudism" T-shirts to the waiting crowds.

After the parade, the masqueraders gather at a big traffic circle and dance late into the night. *Rara* bands with drums, bamboo stalks and a variety of horns made of soldered tin cans, rattles, shakers, pans and other home-made instruments—a testament to Haitian ingeniuity and musical genius—dance from house to hotel making their ancestral music.

Haiti's carnival is made from nothing by people who have nothing. Their unpretentious creative imagination is so strong that from bits of string, cardboard, a little paint and some tin cans they create their own music and their incredible home-made carnival that bubbles with life and joy. Haiti is a country where life and joy do not come easily. Yet—as is so often the case—the poorest put on the best show. A popular saying on this enchanted island is, "Bon temps pas paradies"–"good times not paradise."

Fat Tuesday in New Orleans

A few hundred miles away from this poorest of countries lies the richest of countries. New Orleans hosts America's biggest and most extravagant carnival, appropriately billed as *The Greatest Free Show on Earth*.

The Mardi Gras celebrations in the French Louisiana territories were modelled after the Parisian carnival. When the Spanish took over the French colony in 1766 the tradition was already well established. The rigid Spaniards tried to abolish the custom but with little success.

The port of New Orleans had a reputation for rowdiness and violence, and its street carnival reflected that reputation. The creoles or white French planters withdrew from the wild street celebrations and retreated to their mansions and their society masquerade balls. When America made the Louisiana Purchase in 1803 the territory

78

The procession of the Mystick Krewe of Comus, 23
New Orleans, 1858

was invaded by the wealthy North Eastern Establishment. The prudish Protestant Anglo-Saxons disapproved of New Orleans as a whole and of carnival in particular. They were snubbed by the notoriously snobbish French who refused to admit the Yankees into their society. As more and more Americans flooded the territory the French creoles became increasingly aloof and exclusive in their carnival celebrations which had become a season for lavish social affairs and debutant balls for the elite.

The only refined festivities that were open to the wealthy northerners were the high priced "Bals de Cordon Bleu" or Quadroon Balls, which were revived after the departure of the Spaniards. The Spanish, extreme

racial purists, had banned them during their occupation. These lively balls featured beautiful quadroons, fair skinned girls of less than a quarter black blood, who were double victims of racism, shunned by both whites and blacks. At the Quadroon Balls gentlemen of means, usually creoles, selected poised, well educated mistresses for long-term affairs to supplement their own loveless marriages. French creole society had its own cast system in which marriages were often arranged as liaisons of economic or social convenience. During carnival, the Quadroon balls offered an atmosphere of revelry even the proper gentlemen of Eastern society could not resist.

By the late 1820's the street carnival had also recovered from the Spanish prohibitions and regained its wild momentum. For want of their own tradition, Americans began to join in and eventually dominated the festivities. To compete with the French aloofness they organized their own social season featuring equally exclusive balls and coming-out parties for their own porcelain skinned debutantes. The French tradition of high society snobbery and exclusiveness, which today still characterizes the official carnival in New Orleans, was preserved. In 1838 the first formal street parade was held with decorated carriages, bands and all the classical carnival characters. Perfumed pellets were thrown into the crowds along with flour balls that burst, covering their targets with heavy odours and white dust. Some of these missiles were harmless, others more sinister containing quick lime which caused terrible skin burns. However, this dangerous sport was soon banned.

By the mid 19th century carnival in New Orleans basked in the same glory the festival enjoyed universally. Thousands of balls were held throughout the city. The street celebrations were mad orgies of drunkeness and fighting. Racist red necks, mostly immigrant Irish, would amuse themselves by hunting and beating up blacks, a pathetic sport known as "get niggers". Under the guise of masks, quite a number of murders were committed.

The prostitutes held their own parade. Dressed in outrageous costumes, they would invade the fashionable neighbourhoods shouting obscenities from their carriages at the shocked well-to-do citizens. The ritual battle between winter and spring would be fought by high class uptown whores and their poorer working sisters from the Basin Street red light district.

Basin Street, the birthplace of American jazz, was a seamy section of town. The masked balls held in this area were wild and orgiastic. One of these infamous balls was reported to have a very strict code of dress for its guests. The masquerade was limited to a face mask and, if necessary, a weapon discreetly strapped under a bare armpit. Many adventuresome gentlemen, tired of the formal society affairs staged by their stuffy peers escaped to Basin Street for more lively diversion. Carnival again plunged into chaos.

In 1857 a new parade was introduced which was to change the face of the New Orleans Mardi Gras, or *Fat Tuesday* as it is also known. As if to dramatize the hellish turn the street festivities had taken, the theme presented by the two floats of the new parade was Milton's "Paradise Lost". The "Mistick Krewe of Comus", a secret society whose members introduced the novelty of floats, gave the New Orleans carnival the form it has today. The Civil War dampened the spirit of the celebration, but not for long. The New Orleans society made haste to form exclusive "Krewes", as they called their secret organizations. Each year new floats and new "Krewes" appeared.

In 1871 the Grand Duke Alexis Romanoff of Imperial Russia visited the New Orleans Mardi Gras, causing a furor and inspiring yet another "Krewe" and even the theme song of the New Orleans carnival. According to accounts of the day, the Grand Duke was not at all impressed by the mock royalty, nor by "Rex", the new King of Carnival, inspired by his visit. He refused to sit on a garishly pompous throne the city had especially constructed for him. He found the satirical floats that followed "Rex" and his "Bœuf Gras" with caricatures of President Grant, Lincoln and himself even less amusing. His sense of humour was strained to the limit when the theme song, "If ever I cease to love" was parodied and included an allusion to his rumoured faltering romance with the show girl who had first sung the song to the Grand Duke in New York. Stone faced, Alexis turned his back on New Orleans leaving behind the show girl, the theme song and "Rex", the King of Carnival.

The impudent irreverence suffered by the Grand Duke was mild, however, in comparison to the political parodies that became more obvious in the years following the Civil War. Sometimes floats were stopped by angry crowds. In 1877 the "Mystick Krewe of Comus" chose Hades as the theme for their Mardi Gras floats. Beelzebub bore a striking resemblance to President Grant, and the demonic world of Hades included members of his cabinet and various other politicians. The floats caused a wave of outrage and so incensed the administration that an official protest was issued by Washington. After the incident political allusions faded entirely from the New Orleans Mardi Gras.

Today the allegorical floats and the society balls sponsored by each of the "Krewes" are the main attractions of official carnival. Membership in these societies or even admission to their balls is not open to the public. The "Krewes" are private clubs whose members are carefully screened, and under no circumstances are blacks, Jews, or people of questionable background admitted. The coveted titles of King and Queen are awarded with great care and deliberation. The crown carries such prestige that the lucky Queen can greatly enhance her standing in the New Orleans society. The titled nobility can even assure her a fortunate liaison with an eligible young man of impeccable family background and social standing. The Kings, however, are stoically sworn to secrecy and must wear their titles mutely behind their royal masks. The King's moment of glory comes when he is on his royal float waving regally to the peasants far below, while his entourage of dukes and pages throws millions of dollars worth of plastic coins, jewelry, bracelets, beads, junk novelties, and the occasional real doubloon or coin specially minted to commemorate each "Krewe's" Mardi Gras float. The people fight like children over the worthless treasures in hope of finding a real commemorative doubloon. Not quite the heated gold coins thrown to the Parisian peasants by the French aristocracy, but highly prized collectors' pieces, nonetheless.

The "Krewes" have special days for their parades which begin in January and culminate on Fat Tuesday. On this final day the "Rex Parade" is the main event. The "Rex Krewe" is more liberal than most. The title of "Rex" is not kept secret and is bestowed as a high civic honour. Membership in the "Rex Krewe" is open to upstanding citizens of the community, however, it still bars blacks.

On Fat Tuesday another float appears following "Rex", its King hails from Africa. The Zulu float is the black community's mocking revenge on the high society carnival put on by the exclusive "Krewes" of New Orleans. The Zulu parade is a hilarious drunken parody of "Rex's" pompous pageantry, showing once again that it is the poorest with the least resources who succeed in capturing the spirit of carnival.

The tradition was started at the beginning of this century and the first king wore a tin can for a crown and held a banana stalk for a scepter. Today his face is blackened and he wears leopard skins like an African king. He is attended by his entourage which includes the "Big Shot", representing Africa's wealth, a witch doctor and a host of natives wearing long black underwear and grass skirts. Instead of handing out plastic junk, the Zulu parade offers coconuts. Unlike the Queens of the high society "Krewes", the Zulu Queen is chosen by the King himself and is usually his girlfriend. The title is just as prestigious and coveted as that of any of the white "Krewes". Once when the Zulu king dared not strain the delicate relationships with his various female companions he chose a male impersonator to play the role of his queen, creating the character called "Corinne the Queen".

The Zulu parade, true to carnival spirit, never seems to follow a planned route, it is forever stopping and starting again in an atmosphere of comic drunken disorder. The higher class black community frowns on the shameful Zulu procession, viewing the parody as a degrading racial slur. They have even appealed to black civil rights organizations to ban the Zulu parade outright. But the tradition lives on and has even been enhanced by the presence of renowned musicians, such as Louis "Satchmo" Armstrong, the great jazz man. The Zulu parade is usually led by Pete Fountain, the dixiland jazz clarinetist, and "Olympia", the "Half-fast marching band".

After the monarchs of the "Mystick Krewes" have had their fun flinging trinkets to the crowds, the crowning event of the social carnival season is staged at the giant civic auditorium. This is the "Rex Ball" where the 82 court of "Rex" pays homage to the court of "Comus", the first carnival "Krewe". It is a very formal pompous event with ties and evening gowns, oozing etiquette and snobbery in the French tradition. The down-to-earth revelers who prefer the street carnival, describe it as the "wrecks' ball where you bore your ass off."

While the New Orleans high society prance at their prestigious affair, the "Vieux Carré" is seething with madness and drunken decadence. Thousands of people stumble through the litter of beer cans and paper cups, blowing plastic horns, smoking dope, shouting, whistling, and hugging each other in a bizarre milling ritual. The police round up anybody they find weaving in their direction. Outrageous drag queens, or transvestites, strut around showing off their incredible costumes and their remarkably voluptuous feminine features. Dressed like "Baby Dolls", an old carnival prostitute masquerade, they posture on street corners flaunting and flirting. The homosexual community has completely taken over carnival in the "Vieux Carré". On Mardi Gras they hold their spectacular annual Drag Queen Competition, and they are apparently the only people who are truly seized by the spirit of mask and fantasy. However bizarre or decadent their exhibitionism may appear, it is the transvestites who really stage the "Greatest Free Show" of the New Orleans carnival.

Carnival in Rio

New Orleans may claim to have the greatest free show on earth, but the most spectacular carnival is without doubt staged by the poor "Favelados" who live in the shanty towns, the "Favelas" that hang from Rio de Janeiro's majestic cliffs. For awesome pageantry, the exhileration of music, song and dance, delirious ecstatic liberation, sensual decadence and chaotic collective madness, Rio's fabled carnival is unrivalled. The ancient spirit of licentious abandon, Bacchanalian frenzy and orgiastic Dionysic cult ritual has surfaced in Rio and appears to have found its home.

Brazil has, to this day, all the classical social and economic conditions that have nurtured and resurrected the gods of antiquity since time immemorial. The master-slave relationship of colonial Brazil has hardly changed since emancipation. The basic iniquities still persist. Brazil is a virtually two-class society—the rich and the poor. A homogenized middle class has not yet evolved.

The vast majority of the population is poor, and the miserable living conditions in the "Favelas" worsen as more and more people stream into the big cities from the interior and the rural north. They flock to Rio, the mecca, only to find themselves in shanty towns, staring down on the fabulous wealth of Copacabana and Ipanema. For them, carnival is the liberator, the equalizer that inverts their social condition and their misery, if only for a few fleeting days.

It is a national holiday when the rich descend from their luxurious heights. The poor join them, clambering down from their precarious cliffside perches to give themselves, heart and soul, to carnival. They come down to show the wealthy and the powerful that the repressed, deprived, exploited "Favelado" is also rich and fabulously so—rich in creative energy and exhuberance, rich in imagination. Each year they work and save, sometimes holding two jobs, one just to pay for carnival. They deny themselves to prove that the next carnival will be even better than the one before and that they can outdo the wealthy and the powerful in song and dance, out on the streets where it counts, in front of the whole world.

The rich descend, seduced by the allure of sensuality, longing for a glimpse of the wicked low life. They escape their opulent boredom by putting on the sacred mask, transcending into the magic world of fantasy. The masquerade in Brazil is called the "Fantasia", and for the "Favelado" it opens the same door as it does for the wealthy, only in reverse, and he enters the forbidden realm of wealth and power. This has not changed since colonial days when the rich would blacken their faces and mime the field slaves while the blacks whitened their faces and parodied their masters.

Brazil's West African slave culture was basically the same as in the rest of the New World except that the masters were Portuguese, not French or Spanish. Portugal was Catholic like its colonial competitors but it was never imbued by the rigid morality of the Spanish or the racism of the French. In comparison, Portugal's colonial empire was quite liberal. Miscegenation was widely practiced. Although African Voodoo, or "Candomble" as it is known in Brazil, suffered the same Catholic repression, the colony was so vast and unmanageable that the Portuguese were more concerned with working the land than remaking the black man's faith. The African gods are still very much alive in modern Brazil.

Unlike their colonial neighbours, the Portuguese included the slaves in their carnival celebrations. Between Christmas and Epiphany, when early carnival was celebrated, the good slaves were set free. In those days the main event was the *Entrudo,* and as was the case in the rest of South America, it was an excessively violent affair. Similar to the Roman carnival battles, water was dumped on masqueraders who were then covered with flour. Balls of wax with vinegar perfume or coloured dyes were thrown. More dangerous missiles caused casualties and provoked fights that often left fatalities. At night small groups of blacks would dress like native Africans and dance through the streets, singing and playing their drums.

Carnival in Rio
1823

24

In 1823, to commemorate the first anniversary of Brazil's independence, the Emperor D. Pedro I founded the "Society of the Knights of Fun". A grand parade was staged featuring imperial coaches, spectacular floats and costumes depicting famous personages of the period. Participation in the pageant was open to all but kept apart from the wild *Entrudo.* The dancing at the Emperor's festivities ranged from the popular waltzes to an occasional risqué polka.

In the mid 19th century the *Entrudo* was banned, but it lived on to the turn of the century when it was replaced by the *Corso,* a kind of *Entrudo* with cars. The rich formed a parade in their automobiles while the public threw confetti, streamers and squirted water at them. Social clubs called "Ranchos" played marches. At night, Rio's high society staged fabulous pageants with floats up to 50 meters in length depicting fantastic allegorical themes. Prominent members of Rio's society wore lavish costumes of kings and queens. These magnificent horse drawn cortèges were illuminated by coloured flares and passed to the strains of classical music.

At the turn of the century carnival began to change. A new kind of sound was emerging. Chiquinha Gonzaga, a composer of "Modinhas", popular sentimental Brazilian songs, wrote a lively march for one of the carnival groups. This march contained African rythms which heralded a completely new direction in carnival music. The "Blocos", carnival clubs that came from the slums and were more like neighbourhood street gangs, quickly adopted the infectiously fast choppy beat. Elements of African dance were combined with the drum rhythms and "Samba" was born. For a time this new music was the source of heated controversy. The repressive government found it much too undignified and tried to prohibit it. But Samba prevailed to become the heart and soul of Brazil's carnival.

In 1928 the first Samba school was founded by a neighbourhood group which met near a local school. To dissociate themselves from the rowdy hooligans of the "Blocos", they decided to call themselves an "Escola de Samba". Today there are hundreds of these Samba schools. Some have become enormous complex organizations with thousands of members who pay dues and each year raise the millions of dollars that evaporate in the four days of Rio's Carnival.

At the core of each Samba school is its musical composition–the Samba. Men of simple origin, usually self-taught musicians, try to distill the essence of carnival into a musical theme. Their efforts have been the single greatest source of traditional Brazilian popular music. Once the samba has been composed and selected, the school's parade is built around it and the monumental year long task begins. Choreography, costumes, floats, themes, endless rehearsals build to a climax of fantasy, song, dance and costumed splendour.

The big parade on the Sunday before Ash Wednesday rolls nonstop from sundown until the last of the great schools has passed some eighteen hours later. Each school is allotted approximately one hour to pass the reviewing stands. These schools, some of which number more than 7000 members, put everything they have into that hour. As they form up at the end of the 1000 meter canyon of crowded stands, it is as if a dam was about to break.

At first a trickle appears–the dam has cracked from the strain. Very formally dressed, the head committee of the school makes its entrance, and salutes the anxious crowds. A float follows giving visual dimension to the chosen allegorical theme which is strictly apolitical, Brazil's generals being notoriously intolerant. The themes are mostly chosen from Brazilian history. Standard bearers and pages follow handing out leaflets with the lyrics of the Samba composition and encouraging the exited crowds to sing along.

Then a spectacularly dressed mistress of ceremonies in an elaborate 18th century hooped gown appears escorted by the master of ceremonies in period costume with

86

powdered wig who gracefully dips and whirls around her in an exaggerated courtly manner. After this initial group has passed, the dam bursts and the school floods into the canyon banked with shouting, singing people. The massive percussion section or "Bateria" roars down in a tidal wave of drums, whistles, triangles, tambourines, shakers, cowbells, huge drums, the "Surdos" which provide the deep bass line, and wheezing "Cuicas". The force of their sound is irresistible. As the huge "Bateria" takes its position in a special section near the judges' box to let the main body of dancers pass, the stands are already on their feet.

First the "Sambistas", virtuoso dancers, appear followed closely by the main dance corps. The "Sambistas" are the most dazzling highlight of carnival. They perform incredible double time change ups, and dipping and cross legged whirling routines, around, above, below and between the legs of their partners who sensually arch their "Bunda" or rear end, pumping their nearly naked torsos in a choreographed display of erotic exhibitionism. Their aerial acrobatic variations on the samba are so breathtaking that the crowds go wild. Dancing and singing ripples through the stands like a flood tide. Rio's fierce police try to control the furor and keep it from spilling into the avenue and inundating the passing dancers. This moment is the true essence of Rio's carnival. In a riot of colour, gyrating, writhing, cos-

tumes, Indians, gladiators, harlequins, fan dancers, African warriors, jesters and beautiful mulata girls wearing tangas and huge headdresses pass in frenzied dance.

They are followed almost anticlimactically by the "Wings" and another huge float. The "Wings", former stars of the Samba school are often older, portly women dancers traditionally dressed in costumes typical of Bahia, the old colonial capital of Brazil. The Bahianas' vitality is inspirational, some samba as hard, if not harder than their younger counterparts.

After the main "Escolas de Samba" have "cut their name in the asphalt", as the local expression puts it, the incredible energy generated by their spectacle spills out into the streets and into the many lavish costumed balls held all over Rio.

The street carnival is a paroxysm of exhuberance and frenzied excess. In many parts of Rio the violence rivals the madness of ancient Rome. The *Entrudo* may have disappeared at the turn of the century, but the unleashed fury of chaos and destruction still claims hundreds of victims. Many die from accidents, murders, drunken falls, fights or stabbings provoked by jealousy. Robberies, rapes and police excesses are common. In the days of more repressive government, many political murders were rumoured to have occurred during carnival. The street carnival is marred by thousands of injuries and thousands of arrests. This is the dark tragic side, "bassa bassa"–wanton destruction–as they say in Trinidad. The malicious spirit of the old mischievous gods in their life and death struggle rears its fearsome head. The spector of death strikes at random demanding the blood of its sacrificial victim caught in the vortex of the mad frenzy.

The frenetic street carnival is over-powering, fluctuating wildly from terror to ecstasy from light to darkness. The only escape, for those who can afford the extravagant price of admission, are the society balls, where Eros lights the fantasies of rich and poor alike. Extravagance is part of the carnival magic and even the poor "Favelado", escaping the street rabble, can enter the forbidden guilded halls of the rich and be received like a king.

There are masquarade ball to suite any extreme in taste. The notorious transvestite ball is so decadent that the prudish government censors still ban photographers in an attempt to preserve Rio's reputation. Other balls are renowned for there opulant elegance, some are more extravagant than chic, still others completely unrestrained. As the evening wears on all semblance of decorum evaporates. Lavish costumes dissolve in the perspiration. Great halls, packed to suffocating capacity, pulsate to non-stop samba music in an orgy of wild dancing, singing, carousing and sporadic exhibitionism.

The "Carioca" woman (native of Rio), becomes a queen, the most beautiful and seductive of creatures lusted after by kings and noblemen. Surrendering to her fantasy, she grinds out her erotic dance. The magic of carnival frees her from mundane reality, just as it has liberated the poor "Favelado" who's shanty overlooks her penthouse.As they transcend the material plane, their carefully constructed self-images crumble, helplessly buried under a ludicrous masquarade. He is the powerful knight in shining armour of her dreams, she his queen. The alchemy of carnival has opened the doors to a forbidden world where for a fleeting instant man catches a glimpse of his essence.

At dawn on Ash Wednesday, that magic glimpse has blurred a bit, the fantasy and the "Fantasia" have grown ragged around the edges. Rio, the sensuous beauty, a bit worn as well, her twilit streets littered with streamers, cans, confetti, drunks, bottles and banners, silently proclaim a Samba danced as never before. Spent bodies nestle in the soft curves of her beaches. Exhausted dreamers mercilessly collide with the harsh daybreak, raise their heavy heads, squint briefly at the rising sun, then slowly turn, dragging their incongruous mottled remains back to the beachfront luxury of Copacabana, back to their Ipanema penthouses, back up the towering hills to the shanties of the "Favela".

On the Threshold of Light

THE ETERNAL CULT OF CARNIVAL

The ritual psychodrama has been acted out, the sacred rites performed, the ancient magic has worked its spell on us. Through orgiastic excess and folly, through the embrace of the opposite within us, through the baptism of frenzied chaos we are reborn, revitalized by the laughter of the gods with whom we have danced and played.

Purged of the tensions and anxieties of our existence, we face life anew, reassured with new hope and expectation for the future in the new cycle. The gods are still alive, we have seen and have been touched by them. Through this communion we have drawn new strength from them. The cult ritual we have performed has charged us with their cosmic power.

For the initiated, the spell cast by carnival is more than superstition, more than frivolous distraction and far more than some primitive throwback to paganism that the Church would leave us believe. The universality and incredible vitality of the classical elements found in the celebration across the ages and throughout the world suggests that this ancient rite is linked to the occult. The magic techniques are locked somewhere in our memory, and since the dawn of time we have repeated them at the same cosmic moment when time stands still and the curtain to the supernatural world is parted.

The breach in dimensions between the old and the new cycle activates that memory and draws us out of our illusion called reality into another dimension, a greater reality, a higher level of consciousness, on to another energy plane. In this state, our innate instincts for freedom are liberated. We discard the bonds of our despotic society, we destroy its illusion of order.

This longing for equality and freedom of expression is deeply rooted in our psyche. As Jung and others have argued, it is buried in our collective primordial memory. It is a recollection of that fabled Golden Age when we were all free and equal, living in paradise among the gods. We still long for that blissful state of communion with nature, our fellow man and the universe. We remember the incredible energy that flowed through us when we were in the presence of the divine spirits. The myth keeps alive that memory, and the cult ritual we perform every year enables us to briefly glimpse that idyllic primal state, that lost paradise where our universe was created.

Now that we have fallen from grace and have lost touch with our Being, with the mystical vision of Oneness, as Nietzsche described it, we cling desperately to the myth, our last link with the cosmic forces. In this myth the ancients have hidden the secrets of creation, the key to the magic dimension between time, where life began.

The ritual dictated by the myth is a sacred recreation of that primeval time in which we

89

25
The Golden Age
1573

too were supernatural beings. When we act out the roles in the magic drama, we enter the realm of the gods. Our power is supreme, under the spell of carnival the petty intrigues of our civilization and the inane struggles of what we call the real world appear ludicrous. The inanity and absurdity of our mundane reality, our fanatical preoccupation with power, money, war, weapons, political structures and appearances reduces us to laughter. With scornful derision we dismiss the lies, tear down the veil of pretense, expose the venality and hypocrisy of our civil tyrants, and mock their oppressive authority. We ridicule the politicians who sell us illusion and who enslave us in their industrial paradise. We collectively vent our hostility and suspicion, scorning their 20th century gods: science, technology and money.

To flaunt our disrespect, we extravagantly throw away millions on frivolity in the few short days of celebration. Just as our ancestors called out their priest-kings at the end of the year to account for their ineptness and faltering power, we now call out the modern day politician-magicians and question their failure to live up to their promises for the good and bountiful life. We don the powerful masks of the gods, point our accusing finger and exercise our right of public justice. We call on the ancestral spirits to rise and right the injustices in the social order, injustices caused by these modern kings. We suspect, as our ancestors before us suspected, that their weak magic can no longer bring back the sun and revive life. We see that their modern gods threaten us with extinction, so we dismiss them, turning back to the ancient gods whose power we know innately.

The old gods can bring down the structure that civilization so desperately props up with its armies, doctrines, religions and laws. Carnival is the enemy of form, pretence, and appearance. With its laughter it crumbles the facade of social structure, politics and reason that is so bogged down by form. Because of this destructive spirit the Church and state have always opposed the myth, especially where the tensions created by their arbitrary forms strain the social fabric.

Cult destroys the illusion of structure, mocks the feeble power of the ordered world, dissolves conventions, rigid morality, ideology and norms into total chaos, and demolishes the barriers of age, sex, wealth, title, all the oppressive elements of structured society, plunging us, in the words of M. Eliade, into the "pre-Creation chaos" in which man and element were one.

Having aired our grievances, mocked the illusion of official authority with our laughter and demonstrated our collective disregard for it, we have neutralized the tensions inherent in our social order. The inequities and conflicting elements are reconciled and we rebuild the order and revitalize the community. Just as the ancients performed ceremonies to stimulate the cycle of death and resurrection by simulating the chaos from which life springs, we destroy our world to build it anew.

In the destruction of the social order the individual is lost, swallowed up by the collective. We become disorientated, enchanted by the spell, and, mimicking the divine gestures of the gods, we dance the magic step, drink the sacramental potion, eat the food of the gods, make the ritual sounds, work the ceremonial instruments, put on the sacred mask and become transformed. We are no longer ourselves, freed from the bonds of appearance and identity we are released like the trapped souls of the dead. We tap the mystical powers of the gods and our will is irrepressible. No earthly mortal power can contain us. We become transmuted unstable elements, mercurial. Our reality no longer exists. The laws of man and of nature are suspended.

Through the alchemy of mask, music, dance and drink we gain access to the supernatural. To stimulate the magic we abandon ourselves to the unconscious, formless, asymmetrical, dissonant, disorientated world, where our perceptions are confused and the senses are liberated. Only in madness and chaos are the secret energies of the ancients released.

The cult ritual of carnival creates the necessary conditions to stimulate that release. The noise, the music which fluctuates between the harmonious and the dissonant, the irregular cadence of the drums and the off key brass bands confound our sense of hearing. The sacred dance and its asymmetrical step, stopping, then starting again, disturbs our natural rhythm. The visual elements of carnival shock our sensibilities, confusing our sense of perspective with huge and monstrous creations. The presence of the opposite sex awakens our lust, and the grotesque characters that emerge, the witches, demons and wild creatures with their repulsive physical deformities, disorientate our perception, troubling our emotions with fear and revulsion.

In this disorientated state, great energy is released in us, we awaken another level of consciousness that activates our memory of that distant Golden Age where we were able to harness the cosmic forces and create the great wonders of ancient civilizations, the many marvels that our sophisticated science has still not been able to explain to this day.

In this ecstatic state of trance we feel some small part of that force that gives us the power to continue for days without interruption. It releases a creative force within us that generates the power of the celebration. Construction, composition, choreography, poetry, drama, dance, mime and music are all inspired by this spirit. As Nietzsche maintained, the cult of carnival and the myth from which it springs, have been the source of what we call the "performing arts".

In the context of ritual, art is a collective process. There are no individual creators, no personalities, prices or recognition. There is no distinction between art and artist, actor and audience. All are one and the same. The performance would continue even if no one filled the stands or paid the promoters. The creation is anonymous as are the masked actors presenting it, and it fulfills our need for fantasy.

The battle of Carnival and Lent   26
Peter Brueghel 1559

Much of this creative energy exists as the fusion of opposites, the symmetrical and the assymmetrical, the harmonious and the dissonant. This fusion is the heart of carnival. We cannot resist its attraction because it reveals the opposing forces within ourselves. It is the cosmic principal of energy, the universal prime mover found in Marx's thesis and antithesis, and in the Yin-Yang concepts of Oriental philosophy. Carnival fuses good and evil, the Yin and the Yang, the cosmic duality of the elemental forces, symbolized in the ritual battles and the two-faced divinities. It connects life with death, and realizing that our existence is limited, we make the most of the time between beginning and end. The ancient two-faced gods, Dionysus, the Roman Janus, the Celtic Cernnunos-Esus, still have the power to reveal our own duality; to liberate our repressed fantasies, to expose the dark side of our being.

For some of us this other side our alter-ego is a playful figure, a prankster, symbolized by the archtypal carnival characters, the harlequins and fools that are also locked in our collective memory. For others, the erotic takes over and we abandon ourselves to Eros. In some of us the sinister surfaces, repressed violent emotions erupt. Just as the collective fantasy yields to its destructive elements and inverts the social order, demons within us take possesion and strike out. Evil spirits lurk in the milling madness of the carnival crowds; in this primal darkness anything can happen. Brought face to face with the repressed side of our spirit, we experience what the Greeks called "Catharsis", spiritual purgation, we exorcize the evil demons, are cleansed and emerge whole.

This surfacing from darkness to light lifts our spirits to ecstatic heights of joy. Like children living their fantasy, we jubilate deliriously, relieved of all responsibility. Our innermost longing to be something else, to escape our outer shells, is fulfilled. The powerful magic of the mask enables us to change shape, to laugh at ourselves, and to reestablish contact with our own being. We laugh at the folly of our existence, relieving the tedium, the routine, the boredom of our daily lives. We are renewed by our extravagance and our disregard for the restraints within ourselves and our society. The laughter reveals that the joy of our existence, the ecstatic delights of life, come from beyond this absurd world and its false illusions, beyond the hollow promises of a technological paradise.

The explosive exhuberance, the exhileration, the devastating frenetic excitement of our annual affirmation of life is an expression of our indomitable will to live. This eternal delight of our existence we owe to ourselves, we experience it collectively in the renewed sense of Oneness. The cult magic reconfirms our link to the cosmos, to the supernatural from where our energy flows —and it is a link we have banned from our naively technical conciousness for all too long.

Our civilization has buried our gods with religion, our reason has buried religion with science, promising to make the earth flow with milk and honey. We laugh at them knowing that only the ancient gods can perform these miracles. Just as the Church for centuries promised to return us to the mythical state of grace if only we abandon our pagan gods, now science assures us that we no longer need the old gods, that the sun has been replaced by the atom that the mysteries of nature can be created artificially—and again we laugh. We stand on the brink of chaos assured that the ancient gods will prevail and their cosmic laughter will revive us.

"All our hopes centre on the fact that underneath the hectic movement of our civilization there dwells a marvelous power, which arouses itself mightily only at a certain grand moment then sinks back to dream again of the future."

FRIEDRICH NIETZSCHE

Nadie se conoce

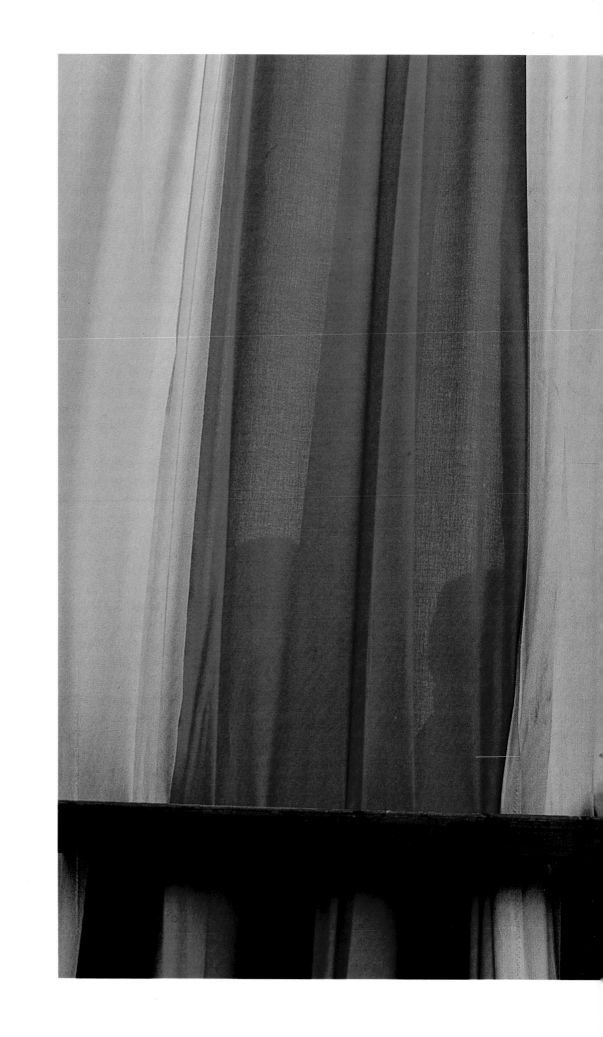

4

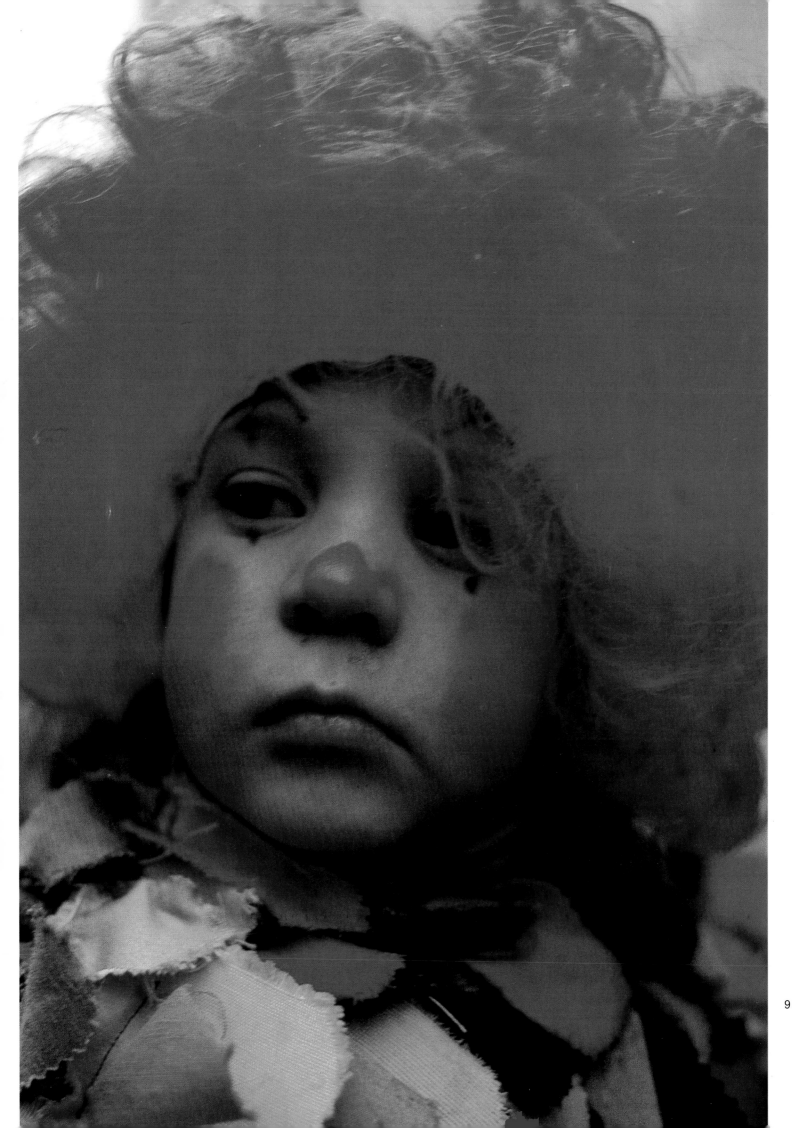

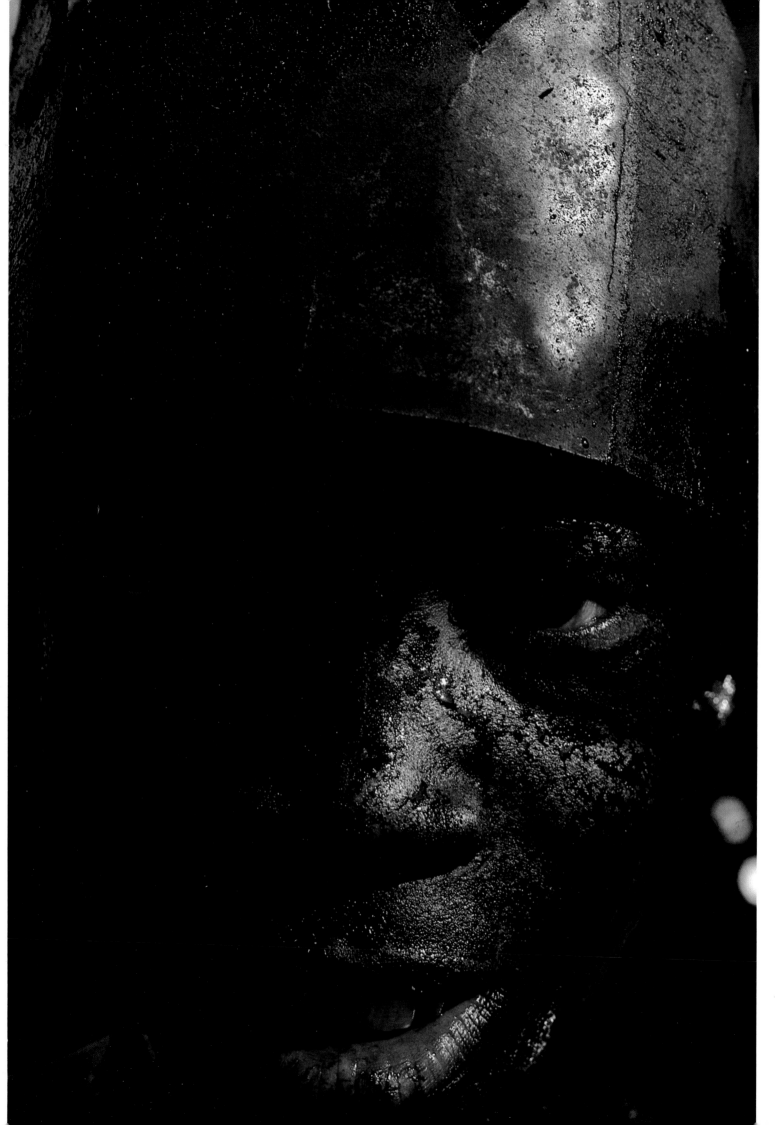

12

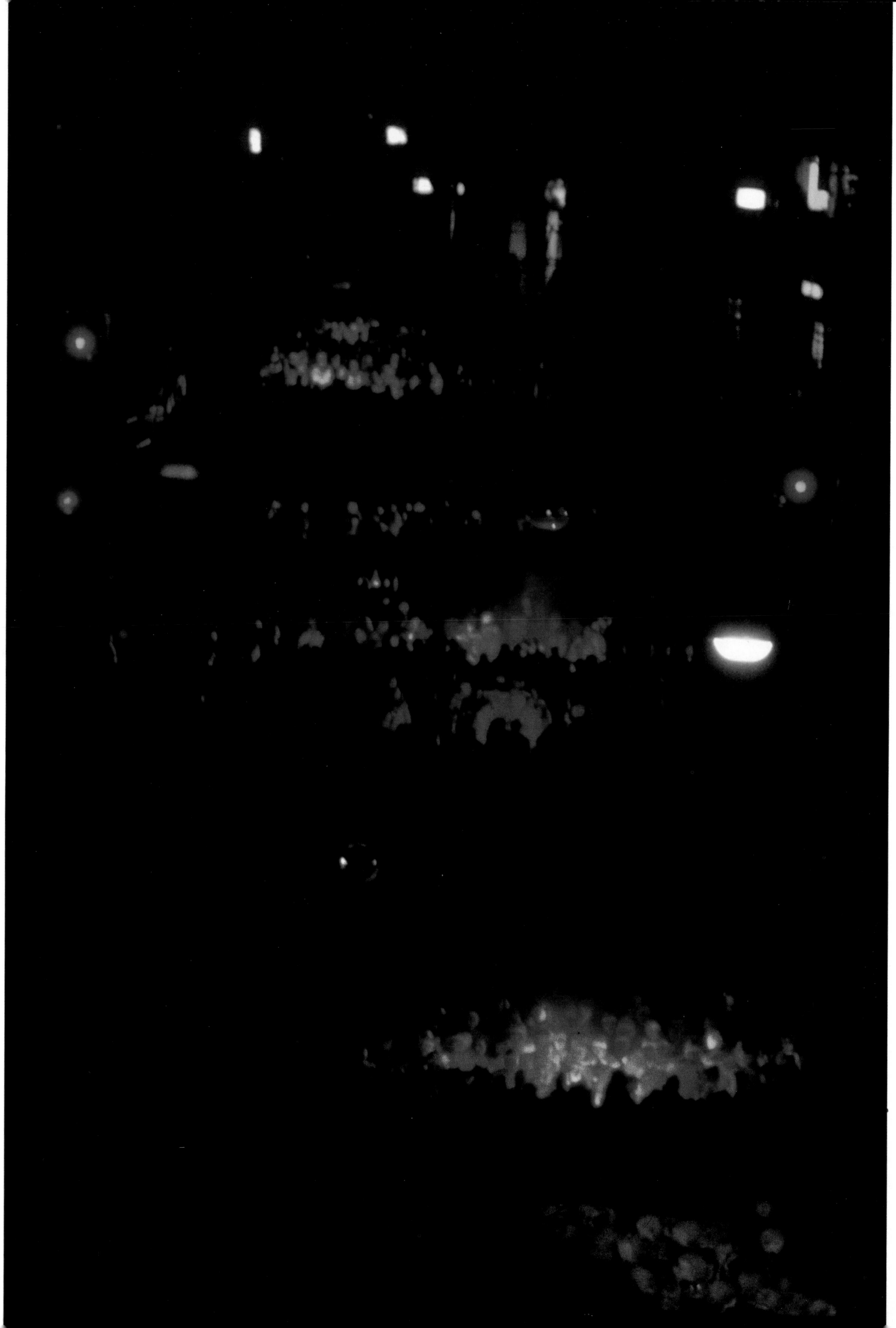

16

17

19

21

23

27/28/29

33

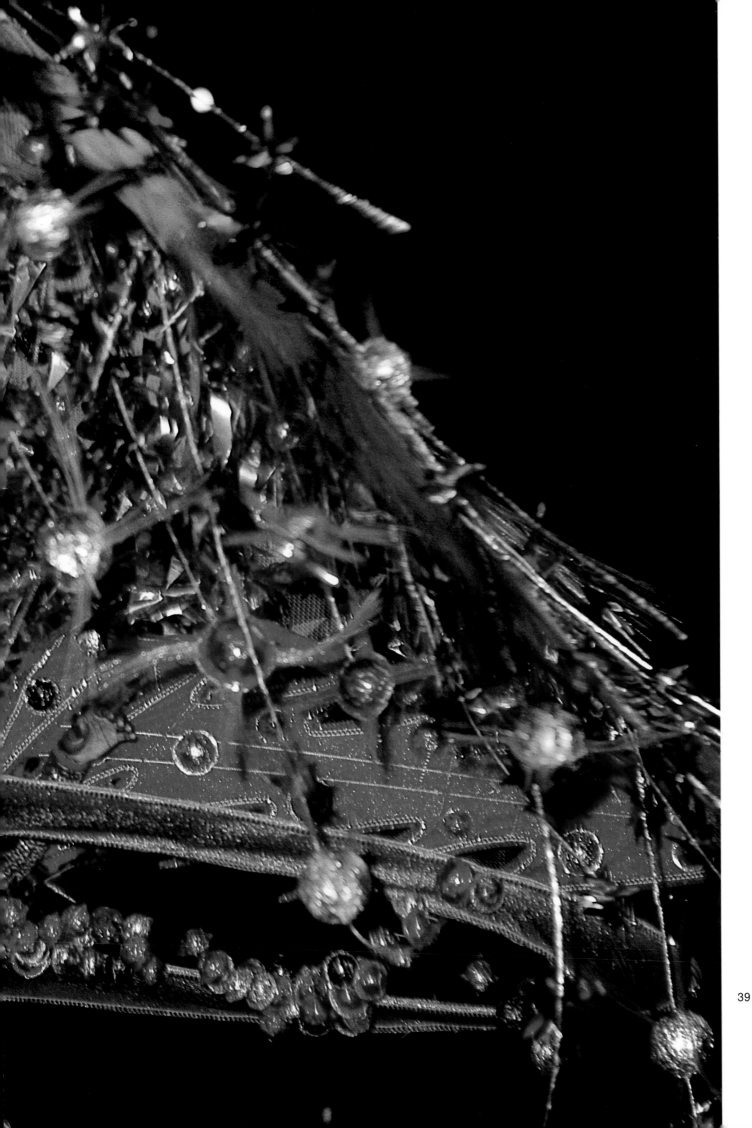

39

46

50

59

61

72

74

85

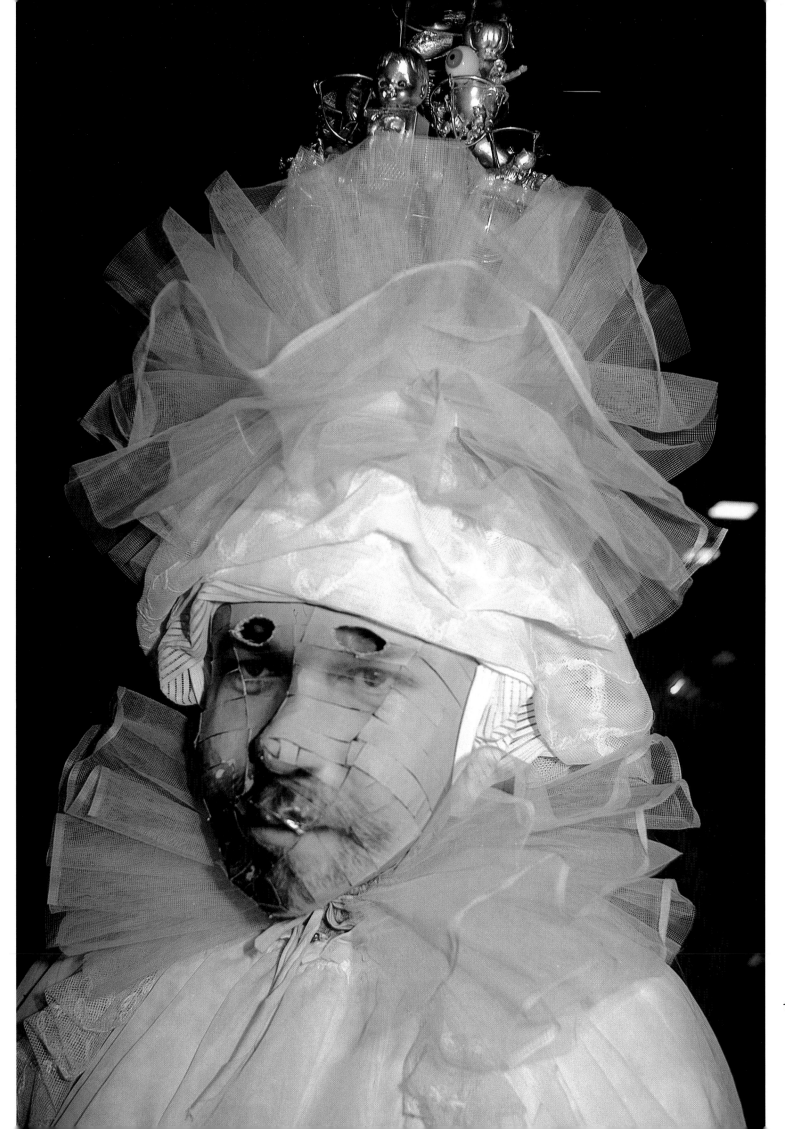

120

List of Plates

Nadie se conoce–No one recognizes anyone
Francisco de Goya, from the series of etchings,
"Los Caprichos", 1798

THE CHILDREN OF CARNIVAL

1 The curtain to the supernatural is parted by a young Cologner. Behind this curtain lies the world of carnival, a magical dimension that awakens the child in us, allowing our fantasies and dreams to become reality.

2 Most carnivals usually reserve special days and events for children's festivities. But many children want to participate in the street carnival of the adults as well like this fiery young carioca who already has Samba in her blood.

3 In Cologne, children, families and friends often dress in similar costumes–like this pair in tattered rag costumes–and then roam the streets of the city in groups.

4 Children watching Basel's "Guggemuusig" Parade are closely supervised by a matronly grandmother.

5 Trinidad, a melting-pot of nations and cultures, has created one of the world's most imaginative and colourful carnivals. Traces of Oriental, Near Eastern, African, Asian and European influence are evident, as can be seen in the face of this small girl.

6 In Binche, the Monday before Mardi Gras is Children's Carnival, when traditional children's groups, like this troupe of Pierrots, make their appearance accompanied by their parents.

7 In Mazatlán, Mexican children also have their own carnival with elaborate floats, a large parade through the city and even a Queen of Carnival Competition.

245

8 The Baslers say that their young are born with the beat of the unique coffee grinder cadence–but do these children know it?
9 During carnival many things are inverted, the old become young and the young often assume a very adult air of haughtiness–like this young Cologner.

10 Haiti's carnival is very spontaneous, especially for the children for whom a simple cardboard mask is often enough to light their fantasies.
11 A young Haitian boy, smeared black with soot and grease, wearing a tin can for a crown venerates his ancient African ancestors.

12 Mexican families come from miles around to participate in the carnival of Mazatlán.
13 An exhausted Trinidadian dracula sheds his bat wings to the delight of his two more energetic friends who immediately claim the prized rolling costume.

14 Kali, the Hindu goddess of destruction, competes in Trinidad's Children's Mas King and Queen Competition.

THE GRAND PAGEANTRY

15 Like ancient pagan tribes performing their sacred dance around the Bengal fires, the Gilles of Binche converge on the town square for their Mardi Gras grand finale.
16 Dawn breaks over one of Rio's huge Escolas de Samba as the last of these big Samba schools passes the judges' stand some 18 hours after the start of the grand parade the previous afternoon.

17 One of the marvels created by Viareggio's "Maghi" mercilessly charicaturizes the world's political leaders as just so many puppets on strings.
18 A "Carrus Navalis" of incredible proportions ridden by a giant Pierrot sails through the crowds of Viareggio.

19 Nice's huge papier mâché king, "His Majesty King Carnival", and his entourage of follies pass the grand stands.

20 The inhabitants of the Kaygasse in Cologne have fitted out a whole flock of birds to parade in the "Schull- und Veedels-Zög" through the narrow streets of the old city.

21 In Nice, a giant mechanical float depicts the terrifying perils of the jungle.

22 In Viareggio, a huge buffoon satirizes the perils of modern civilization where fools weigh our lives against missiles and bombs.

23 A Viking ship, similar to the sacred ship of the mythological Norse god Frey, ploughs its way through the carnival revelry of Mazatlán, shooting fireworks from its bow.

24 Fireworks cascade over the heads of one of Binche's traditional groups, the "Peasants", as they dance the final rounds in front of the Bengal fire.

25 Under a huge likeness of the Brazilian mermaid sea goddess Iemanja, Bahianas in traditional costumes of Northern Brazil prepare for their moment of glory before the reviewing stands.

26 A dancer enthusiastically whirls her hooped gown to the beat of Samba music, cutting her name in Rio's asphalt.

27
28 Samba, the heart of Rio's carnival, is a display of sensuality and eroticism, a modern version of an ancient lust-inducing fertility
29 dance.

30 Trinidad's famous King and Queen of Carnival Competitions
31 inspire the most incredible costumes. Here an oriental god of thunder dances across the stage followed by a woman dressed as the contents of a bursting Christmas wrapping.

32 Lost in the whirlwind of ecstatic dance, this joyous Trinidadian gypsy flashes her exuberant smile.

33 During Nice's "Corso", the Sun King, "Roi Soleil", spreads his arms in greeting.
34 This golden lotus on wheels rolls across the stage. The strict rules of Trinidad's King and Queen of Carnival Competition require that all masqueraders be able to move and even dance in their huge costumes without assistance.

35 Rio's carnival is for everyone, and the fever of Samba takes possession of even the most severely handicapped.
36 The "Sambistas" are the most dazzling highlight of Rio's carnival. Their acrobatic variations on the Samba are so breathtaking that the crowds go wild.

37
38 During the 60 minutes allotted to each of Rio's Samba schools for their performance, the dancers, musicians and spectators put their heart and soul into the spectacular parade, especially if they have managed to reach the grand stands and the glaring lights of the television cameras.

39 Like some cosmic storm, meteors, shooting stars and bolts of lightning come crashing down around the head of this exhausted and disappointed masquerader whose over-ambitious costume crumbles because of structural flaws. This competitor was disqualified from Trinidad's King of Carnival Competition.

40 After the Escolas de Samba have passed the grand stands, the tremendous energy they generate carries the dancers into the streets of Rio.
41 In Mazatlán, traditional Mexican folk dances are performed on stages set up in the many squares of the city.

42 Surrounded by the "Grosses Têtes" of French origin, this Haitian Charlie Chaplin dances a jig in the streets of Port au Prince.
43 For "Weiberfasnacht", an older "Tanzmariechen" dressed in the uniform of the "Rote Funken" does a dance during the opening of Cologne's street carnival.

TRADITION

44 The members of Basel's snake clique, whose Fasnacht theme always incorporates snakes in their masquerade, parade in Medusa costumes, Medusa being one of the most terrifying characters of Greek mythology. Her hair consisted of snakes and anyone who dared look at her was immediately turned to stone.
45 A fifer and drummer wind their way down one of Basel's ancient back streets.

46 Basel's grand finale falls on the Wednesday after Ash Wednesday when all the cliques don their grotesque masks and parade through the streets of the city.
47 The Gilles of Binche wear their masks only on the morning of Mardi Gras when they descend on the town hall to claim the city.

48 In the twilight of Mardi Gras, Binche's Gilles throw the last of their oranges, symbols of the sun, to the crowds.
49 This Basler fifer, artistically disguised as the sun, winds his way through the narrow alleys of Basel. The unwritten rule of masquerading in Basel requires that the entire body be disguised.

50 One of Basel's many cliques, dressed in traditional costumes,
51 marches through the narrow alleys in the old part of the town while a lone drummer marches to the beat of the stuttering coffee grinder cadence for which the Basler drummers are renowned.

52 During "Schleicherlaufen", the Tyrolean "Laternenträger"
53 dances through the streets of Telfs, gracefully swinging his lantern, clearing the way for the "Schleicher", the incarnations of spring. Wearing their youthful masks and attired in fantastic costumes with symbols of fertility, the "Schleicher" banish winter with the booming sound of their bells.

54 After they have danced their final round and the huge cowbells have sounded for the last time, the exhausted "Schleicher" remove their incredible heavy hats and return home.

55 In a meadow outside Telfs, the bear hunters return with the bears who symbolize the captured winter. This ritual bear hunt is one of Telfs' oldest carnival rituals.

56 The adversaries of the "Schleicher" are the "Wilde Männer". They are also incarnations of winter and wear costumes made of lichen and masks carved from a single piece of wood.

57 Originally these "Wilde Männer" were quite violent. Here they are pulling the cart of one of the heralds of Telfs' Fasnacht, followed by an allegorical cart carrying a house of almost normal proportions satyrizing a local building scandal.

58 The "Wilde Mann" of Basel's "Vogel Gryff" tradition wears a terrifying brass mask and a belt of leaves to which apples are attached. Children who try to snatch at the apples are swept away by the wild man's pine tree.

59 In Cologne, the "Blaue Funken", symbolizing the hated Prussian honor guards, present arms and rears. This is known as "Wibbln", a traditional parody of the military.

60 Masks worn by members of a "Guggemuusig" band called "Träne-Furzer" (farting tears) lie laughing in the streets, as tired Baslers stop for a drink in a nearly tavern.

THE STREETS

61 A fat mamma postures proudly for a New Orleans policeman.

62 After the opening of "Weiberfasnacht", Cologne's emancipated women surround a policeman and shower him with wet lipstick kisses.

63 With a serious expression on his face, this clown observes the hectic activity of the "Schull- und Veedels-Zög" on the street below.

64 On "Rosenmontag" the streets of Cologne are packed with spectators, some of them are masked for the occasion but not really touched by the spirit of carnival.

65 One of Basel's large "Guggemuusig" bands parade as Arab sheiks. All senses are confused by the shrill dissonance of their loud, off-key refrains which deteriorate to cacophony then finally pick up the melody again.

66 "Back to belly", this Trinidadian couple shuffles along keeping time to the music.
67 At dawn, on the morning of "Jouvay", a Trinidadian Steel Pan Band surrounded by dancing and singing revelers is pushed through the streets of Port of Spain.

68 In the dusty late afternoon another Steel Pan Band slowly cuts through the throngs of people after Trinidad's Mas Band Competition.
69 In Haiti, many carnival guises remind one of ancient African customs. In Port au Prince this African face, beautifully painted in the manner of West African ritual, peers out of the crowd.

70 Unable to restrain herself, a woman breaks out of the crowd to
71 join one of Nice's fools for a few steps of dancing during the "Corso". Behind them a carnival group invited from Germany marches in traditional grotesque masks carrying inflated pork bladders said to contain the souls of the dead. The "Grosses Têtes", on the other hand, are traditional figures of Nice's carnival. They roam through the crowds throwing confetti.

72 During carnival in Cologne one often sees serious faces, and it is
73 not always exhaustion that excludes them from the joyous atmosphere of carnival. Many masqueraders are not able to become entranced just by wearing a mask. No matter how clever or imaginative their costume may be, they remain mere onlookers in the world of magic surrounding them.

74 This yellow-faced Haitian sandwich-man wearing a large cardboard hat, is a lawyer. His hat proclaims the years of service dedicated to his profession, and his sandwich board ironically declares his support for carnival, his country, its children, its presidents etc., etc.
75 A pensive Mexican vendor stands beside his last two remaing masks.

The Radiant Elegance or Carnival:
76 A Trinidadian beauty wearing a spectacular headdress.
77 A Mexican folklore dance troop waves from a float.
78 A red lotus flower from Trinidad beams a shy smile.

79 During Nice's famous "Bataille des Fleurs", beautiful young
80 girls, dressed in elegant gowns or as bathing beauties, throw bouquets of flowers to the crowds lining the streets. The traditional flower of carnival is the mimosa which is distributed generously in Nice as well as in Basel and other towns.

Masquerade–the artist's playground:
81 An ancient king from Trinidad.
82 An Inca goddess from Rio.
83 A transvestite butterfly in New Orleans.
84 Stars, stripes and clouds from Trinidad.

85 Cosmic aura is the theme represented by this glittering Mas Band during in Trinidad's Carnival Competition.

86 A giant guiding star illustrates the theme "Christmas", chosen
87 by one of Trinidad's larger Mas Bands, while golden stars illuminate the happy eyes of this girl, one of the members of the Mas Band.

88 The giant Christmas star disappears into the carnival crowd of Trinidad.

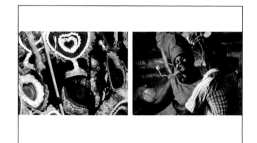

89
90 Trinidad's last lap begins to take its toll. A tired valentine stares vacantly into space while an enthusiastic dancer succumbs to sweet exhaustion in the arms of a friend who helps her off the stage.

THE BIZARRE

91 In the inverted world of carnival where our senses are confused and our perceptions distorted, a youth, mask slung over the back of his head, sits on one of Rio's mosaic sidewalks.
92 A Basler clique takes a break in a nearby tavern while their masks patiently await their return.

93
94 A bizarre she gorilla promenades through the Vieux Carré of New Orleans, while an urban tarzan gives his wild call of the jungle.

95 A phantom army of "Marrons", symbolizing the rebellious slaves of colonial Haiti invades the streets of Port au Prince wearing terrifying teeth and lips.
96 A bizarre Haitian boy, covered with white powder and carrying a broom, scurries through the crowds. The broom, a universal symbol traditional to carnival is used to sweep out winter and all the evil of the past year.

97 This Haitian is spectacularly disguised as an Arawak indian. These indians believed their island to be the cradle of the sun and the moon.
98 A big-lipped warrior leers menacingly. His face has been smeared with black grease like the faces of the "Marrons" who fled into the jungle and formed a resistance movement, finally emerging to liberate Haiti from the French.

99 In Cologne, a blue-faced dracula bares his teeth.
100 These two New Orleans transvestites flash a toothy smile.

101 In the Middle Ages during the Feast of Fools, it was common for laymen to impersonate nuns–a sacrilegious custom that has found its way into the carnival of New Orleans.

102 A New Orleans "Baby-Doll", an old carnival prostitute charac-
103 ter, poses on a street corner of the Vieux Carré while high above her on a balcony, an ancient Egyptian god and his up-to-date companions survey the madness and the decadence of the world below.

104 The inversion of sexes, an ancient carnival tradition, lives on in
105 New Orleans where an annual Drag Queen Contest is held on Mardi Gras.

106 When night falls on carnival the strangest creatures make their appearance, such as this Basler fifer wearing an elaborate yet un-traditional bird mask.
107 Haiti's "Bois Pi-haut" is a horned character of African mytho-logy. However, it also resembles the stag mask of the ancient Celts which was worn for the ritual expulsion of winter.

108 In Haiti, this macabre Grinning Death tries to attract attention with his umbrella.
109 The commercial aspect of carnival is often anything but cheer-ful. In Viareggio this folorn rubber skull waits for a buyer.

110 Carnival, especially at night, is witching time, when witches and phantoms ascend from the realms of the underworld to mingle with the living.
111 In Basel as well, witches try their luck at casting spells on the spectators–to the dismay of the more traditionally-minded Bas-lers who often frown upon costumes that do not conform to the classical Basel Masquerade.

112 At one of Rio's many balls, a red devil lunges with his trident.
113 Sculls hang like trophies from the macabre costume of this Trinidadian. Carnival is a time when the dead spirits rise and mingle with the living to dance the dance of life.

114 An untraditionally costumed Basler peers through the window
115 frame which he carries as part of his costume. And yet another Basler confounds the perceptions with his ingenious photographic mask. Carnival is the time when we do not know whether we are looking into or out of ourselves, when we do not know whether what we see will become visible through our eyes or through the eyes of another.

116 This Basler joker with cards hanging from his fool's cap plays his fife late into the night.
117 A phantom mask illuminated by a tiny lamp breaks the darkness of "Morgenstreich".

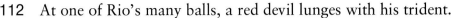

THE LAST LAP

118 A tired masquerader sits on a staircase while a cheerful Basler clique noisily passes by.
119 The "Alte Tante" or "Fasnachtsfrau", the long-nosed busybody, is one of the classical figures of Basel's Fasnacht.

120 While he dances through the streets of Viareggio, a clown, cheered on by the crowds, directs an orchestra.
121 A victim of Basel's infamous "Intrigieren" receires a face full of confetti and an ear full of intrigue.

122 For "Morgenstreich" the Baslers assemble carrying their huge, beautifully painted lanterns.
123 A slightly drunk Binchois, his face as pink as his costume, stares vacantly into the darkness.

124 A portly woman dances the "Tarantella" to the enthusiastic
125 applause of the onlookers while a pair of laughing "Bur-lamaccos", the harlequins of Viareggio, accompany a King along the parade route.

126 Accompanied by a Mexican "Mariachi" band, this reveler sings
127 his heart out to an appreciative audience while a young chaperoned girl takes advantage of the distraction to steal a glance at the young man sitting nearby.

128 Public nudity is forbidden in Rio, even during carnival—but for some this is only a minor technicality.
129 A leering "Hun" sits drinking in one of Cologne's taverns.

130 At one of Rio's fabled masquerade balls, scantily clad
131 "Cariocas" act out their sexual fantasies.

132 Romance and would-be romance in Cologne. The kiss of youth
133 and the remembrance of youth—the magic of carnival eraces all barriers, even age.

134 Under the spell of the sacramental wine, a drunken Bacchus weaves through New Orleans' Vieux Carré.

135 On the morning after Rio's carnival, two straggling indians, be-
136 ings from another world, wait at a bus stop. An exhausted
Trinidadian collapses on the sidewalk supported by his girlfriend.

137 More victims of Trinidad's last lap: lovers rest on their doorstep
138 while further down the street an exhausted warrior passes out
before reaching his own door.

139 Mockingly, Telfs' "Zanger" sticks his long tongue out at us and
lets out the last laugh before disappearing behind the canopy of
his gypsy wagon to await the next carnival.

SOURCE OF ILLUSTRATIONS

Bibliothèque Nationale, Paris: 1, 6, 7, 9, 10, 12, 13, 18, 20, 25

Centro documentario storico del Comune di Viareggio: 19

Columbia University Library, New York: 21 (and end-paper)

Costio Mayo Foundation, Rio de Janeiro: 24

Kunsthistorisches Museum, Vienna: 26 (and front-paper)

Louvre, Paris: 3, 4

Musée de L'Homme, Paris: 2, 8

Musée International du Carnaval et du Masque, Binche: 17

Staatliche Antikensammlungen, Munich: 5

The New York Public Library, New York: 14, 15, 22, 23

Tiroler Landesmuseum Ferdinandeum, Innsbruck: 16

Bibliography

Acosta, A.: El Carnaval y los danzas Carnovalescos, Hemisferio, Mexico, Marzo, 1945.

Allardyce, N.: The World of Arlequin, Cambridge, 1963.

Bademacher, C.: Ancient Shrove-tide customs, International Folklore Congress, Chicago, 1898.

Boroja, C.: Le Carnaval, Paris, 1979.

Campbell, J.: The Mask of God, Primitive Mythology; Creative Mythology, New York, 1959.

Christ, R.: Fasnacht in Basel, Basel, 1960.

Courland, H.: Haiti Singing. New York, 1973.

Davidson, H.: Gods and Myths of Northern Europe, Baltimore, 1964.

Dawkins, R.: The Modern Carnival in Thrace and the Cult of Dionysus, Journal of Hellenic Studies, London, 1906.

Dörer, A.: Das Schemenlaufen in Tirol, Innsbruck, 1938.

–: Tiroler Fastnacht, Wien, 1949.

Elderkin, G.: Studies in Dionysian and Kindred Cults. Princeton, 1924.

Eliade, M.: Myths, Dreams and Mysteries, London, 1960.

–: The Myth of the Eternal Return, New York, 1954.

–: Myth and Reality, New York, 1963.

–: The Sacred and the Profane, New York, 1959.

–: Traite d'histoire des Religions, Paris, 1949.

Eneida: Historia do Carnaval, Carioca, Rio de Janeiro, 1958.

Fabre, D.: Le Monde du Carnaval, Annales ESC nr. 2, 1976.

Fowler, W.: The Roman Festivals, London, 1899.

Frazer, J.: The Golden Bough, London, 1911.

–: The Worship of Nature, New York, 1926.

Fuchs, P.: Kölner Karneval, Köln, 1972.

Gaignebet, C.: Le Carnaval, Paris, 1974.

Gardel, L.: Escola de Samba, Rio de Janeiro, 1967.

Galli, N.: Viareggio, I Carneval: un'altra vita, Firenze, 1978.

Gaster, T.: Thespis, Ritual, Myth and Drama in the Ancient Near East, New York, 1950.

Gennep, A.: Le cycle ceremonial du carnaval et du careme, Paris, 1925.

–: Manuel de Folklore Francais Contemporain, Paris, 1947.

Glotz, S.: Le carnaval de Binche, Gembloux, 1975.

–: Catalogue: Le masque et le carnaval dans le monde, Binche, 1970.

–: Catalogue: Le masque dans la tradition europeene, Binche, 1974.

Goethe: Voyage en Suisse et en Italie, Paris, 1878.

Goldman, A.: Carnival in Rio, New York, 1978.

Gray, L.: The Mythology of All Races, New York, 1944.

Grimm, J.: Teutonic Mythology, Gloucester, 1976.

Guren, J.: Carnival Panorama, New Orleans, 1966.

Hatt, J.: The Celts and Gallo-Romans, London, 1970.

Herman, P.: Unsere Fasnacht, Basel, 1971.

Hill, Errol: The Trinidad Carnival, Austin, 1972.

James, E.: Seasonal Feasts and Festivals, London, 1961.

Klersch, J.: Die Kölnische Fastnacht, Köln, 1961.

La Cour, A.: New Orleans Masquerade, New Orleans, 1952.

Meuli, C.: Les Origines du Carnaval, Annuaire de la Commision Royal Belge de Folklore, vol. 15, 1961–62.

Michelson, H.: Une etude sur le folklore Haitien. Port au Prince, 1954.

Otto, W.: Dionysus, Myth and Cult, Bloomington, 1965.

Pourot, P.: La Chanson, le masque, la danse. Paris, 1927.

Radin, P.: The Trickster, London, 1956.

Rahner, H.: Greek Myths and Christian Mysteries, New York, 1971.

Sidro, A.: Le Carnaval de Nice et ses Fous, Nice, 1979.

Tallant, R.: Mardi Gras, Garden City, 1948.

Thompson, K.: Background of Trinidad's Carnival and Calypso, Port of Spain, 1954.

Toschi, P.: Le Origini del teatro italiano, Torino, 1955.

Trillins, C.: Zulu, Special Aid and Pleasure Club, New Yorker, June 20, 1964.

Vazquez, H.: El Carnaval, Mexico, 1931.

Young, P.: The Mistick Krewe, New Orleans, 1931.

Zimburg, H.: Der Perchtenlauf in der Gastein. Wien, 1947.

Acknowledgements

I would like to express my grateful appreciation to all those, without whose generous help this volume could not have been realized.

For their moral and material support, I would like to thank my parents, the families Kasem-Beg, Haysom, Brui, Frey, Campos and von Schweder, Janet Haysom, Bob Abrams, Sophie Roberte, Inge Geiger-Born, Birgit Haberbosch, Nancy Lees, Tom Tiberii and Ruth Moser.

For their invaluable technical advice and assistance I would like to thank William Brui, Samuel Glotz, Peter Frey, Jerry Joyner, Maurice Seymour, Benedikt Erhard, Jacques Rutten, Deborah Robin, Dolores Miazzo, Sara Nicoll, Josef Härting, Wolfgang Frank and Ernst Born.

The photographs in this book were taken with the Nikon F2, the Nikomat FTN, the Nikomat EL and the Nikon FE. Lenses used: Nikkor 24 mm f 2.8 / 35 mm f 1.4 / 50 mm f 1.4 / 55 mm f 3.5 / 85 mm f 2 / 180 mm f 2.8. Films used: Kodak High Speed Ektachrome (Daylight and Tungsten), Kodachrome X and II, Kodachrome 25 and 64.

Other illustrated volumes published by Perlinger Verlag

Gert Chesi

Voodoo–Africa's Secret Power

276 pages, 128 colour plates, numerous black-and-white photographs. 25 × 30 cm, cloth bound.

The Austrian journalist Gert Chesi spent years of research gathering the photographic and documentary material that has been used to create this remarkable book, the most unique of its kind on West African voodoo, a subject that is beginning to attract the increasing interest of the public. This book gives us a deeper understanding of the Afro-American syncretism that was brought back from America by the slaves of once and spread through Africa in the postcolonial era. More than any other religion, voodoo has been able to restore to the African his lost identity. Published in English, French, German, Swedish and Spanish.

Gert Chesi

The Last Africans

240 pages, 148 colour plates, numerous black-and-white photographs and illustrations. 23.5 × 31 cm, cloth bound. Third, fully revised edition 1981.

In this fascinating illustrated volume, Gert Chesi portrays the traditional life of various African tribes. This book is not only fascinating but also highly informative which is partially due to an additional chapter dealing with African architecture as well as to the numerous sketches, maps and Chesi's brilliant photographs, which have been reproduced perfectly in this book. It is an internationally acknowledged contribution to a better understanding of Africa. Published in English, German, French, Swedish and Spanish.

Gert Chesi / Susanne Wenger

A Life with the Gods

256 pages, 76 colour plates, numerous black-and-white photographs. 25 × 30 cm, cloth bound.

The Austrian artist Susanne Wenger has been living with the Yorubas of Nigeria for 30 years. Their ancient and subtle traditions have become a substantial part of her life. For 30 years she has been studying the behaviour and religious manifestations of these people and, with the help of native artists, she has developed a "New Sacred Art". She describes her own life with the Gods as well as the profound rituals of the Yorubas. Gert Chesi's brilliant photographs and comments put the finishing touch to this unique documentation of one of the most important religious, mythological and social systems of Africa. Published in English and German.

Gert Chesi

Faith Healers in the Philippines

288 pages, 64 colour plates, numerous black-and-white photographs. 25 × 30 cm, cloth bound.

Gert Chesi, the author of "Voodoo", is no novice to the world of spiritualistic phenomena and healing rituals. In this book, he has attempted to illustrate the phenomenon of faith healing, as practiced in the Philippines and well known for the very controversial "bloody operations", from three basically different viewpoints: that of the healers themselves–in what light they regard their own work and that of other healers, both genuine and fake; that of the patients from all over the world whose statements pertain to the success or failure of all kinds of treatment; and finally his own–what he himself experienced in the course of his trips and how he deals with the difficulty, many of the western people have in adapting their rationall-oriented minds to a phenomenon for which they have no logical explanation. Published in English, German and French.

Fritz Trupp

The Last Indians–
South America's Cultural Heritage

264 pages, 144 colour plates, numerous black-and-white photographs and illustrations. 25 × 30 cm, cloth bound.

In this fascinating volume, the Austrian ethnologist Dr Fritz Trupp gives a comprehensive report of the situation of the remaining Indian tribes of South America today. With great empathy for a people whose culture is so totally different from western society, he describes the lives of eight traditional tribes in fascinating detail, from their diet and social structure and their architecture to their religion and magic rites. Trupp has collected his very unique material at an important moment, before the Indian drums are silenced for ever by the lure of western life-styles and the roar of the bulldozer in a fatal combination of misunderstood progress and unadorned rapacity. Published in English, German, French and Spanish.

Perlinger Verlag

A-6300 Wörgl (Austria), Brixentaler Straße 61, phone (0 53 32) 33 41-3 / telex 051/205 teltaz